The Ellen Clarke Bertrand Library
Bucknell University
Lewisburg, Pennsylvania

WOMEN'S SOCIAL STANDING

Also by Roy A. Carr-Hill

BRITAIN'S BLACK POPULATION (*coedited with Ashok Bhat and Sushel Ohri*)
CRIME, POLICE AND CRIMINAL STATISTICS (*with Nick Stern*)
THE DEVELOPMENT AND EXPLOITATION OF EMPIRICAL BIRTHWEIGHT STANDARDS (*with Colin W. Pritchard*)
INDICATORS OF THE PERFORMANCE OF EDUCATIONAL SYSTEMS (*with Olaf Magnussen*)
LES INEGALITES SOCIALES DE LA SANTE EN FRANCE ET EN GRANDE BRETAGNE (*with Pierre Aiach, Sarah Curtis and Raymond Illsley*)
PRIMARY EDUCATION AND WORLD RECESSION (*with Dieter Berstecher*)
SOCIAL CONDITIONS IN SUB-SAHARAN AFRICA

Women's Social Standing

The Empirical Problem of Female Social Class

Roy A. Carr-Hill
Research Coordinator
School of Social and Political Science
University of Hull

and

Colin W. Pritchard
Research Fellow
Social Paediatric and Research Unit
University of Glasgow

St. Martin's Press   New York

© Roy A. Carr-Hill and Colin W. Pritchard 1992

All rights reserved. For information, write:
Scholarly and Reference Division,
St. Martin's Press, Inc., 175 Fifth Avenue,
New York, N.Y. 10010

First published in the United States of America in 1992

Printed in Hong Kong

ISBN 0-312-06868-9

Library of Congress Cataloging-in-Publication Data
Carr-Hill, R. A. (Roy A.), 1943–
Women's social standing / Roy A. Carr-Hill
and Colin W. Pritchard.
p. cm.
ISBN 0-312-06868-9
1. Women—Great Britain—Social conditions. 2. Social classes—
—Great Britain. 3. Great Britain—Occupations—Classification.
I. Pritchard, Colin. II. Title.
HQ1593.C37 1992
305.5'0941—dc20   91–24701
                                                    CIP

Contents

List of Tables viii

Preface xi

Acknowledgements xiii

1 Introduction 1
   1.1 The Relevance of Debates about Class 2
   1.2 Conventional Treatments of Women in the Class Debate 3
   1.3 The Structure of the Book 5

PART I THE GENESIS OF THE CURRENT SOCIAL CLASSIFICATION OF WOMEN

2 The Registrar-General's Social Class Scheme: The Stevenson Version 10
   2.1 Introduction 10
   2.2 Origins of the Social Class Scheme According to Stevenson 11
   2.3 The Ideological Context of a Social Classification: Szreter 17
   2.4 Justifying the Classification 20
   2.5 Concluding Remarks 22

3 The Registrar-General's Social Class Scheme: The Last Half-Century 25
   3.1 Modifications 1931–71 25
   3.2 Classification based on Employment Statistics 25
   3.3 The Proposed Standard Occupational Classification 30
   3.4 A Résumé: Is Stevenson's Social Class Scheme Relevant Today? 31

4 Women in the Social Class Scheme 33
   4.1 Introduction 33
   4.2 The Origins of the Method of Treatment of Women in the Social Class Scheme 33
   4.3 The Mixed Basis for Assigning Women to a Social Class Classification under the SCS 36
   4.4 What if Women Counted? 40

5	**Do Women Marry Socially?**	**44**
	5.1 Marital Social Class	44
	5.2 The Wee Laddie Next Door?	46

PART II CONSTRUCTING A SOCIAL CLASSIFICATION FOR WOMEN

	Prologue	54
6	**Classification Using HORG and the Alternative**	**56**
	6.1 Technical Criteria for an Index	56
	6.2 The Options	61
	6.3 Height, Fertility and Infant Mortality	64
7	**Measuring Female Life Chances: The Variables and the Data**	**67**
	7.1 What Kind of Outcome Measures are Appropriate?	67
	7.2 Measuring the Good Life	69
	7.3 The Data Available	70
	7.4 Variables and Data for Quality of Life Indicators	71
	7.5 The Empirical Comparison of Discrimination	73
8	**The Distribution of Female Life Chances**	**75**
	8.1 Introduction	75
	8.2 Contemporary Data on Health	76
	8.3 Learning	80
	8.4 Material Possessions	82
	8.5 Lifestyle	83
	8.6 Relating	86
	8.7 Prognosis	88
	8.8 Historical Data on Health	89
	8.9 Historical Data on Lifestyle	93
	8.10 Historical Data on Relating	93
	8.11 Historical Data on Prognosis	95
	8.12 Conclusion	

PART III WHAT ROLE DOES HEIGHT PLAY?

	Prologue	100
9	**A Tall Story**	**101**
10	**The Role of Height**	**108**
	10.1 Height as an Indicator of Development	108
	10.2 Height and Adult Health (Behaviour)	109

10.3	Height and Social Inequalities	113
10.4	Height: An Environmental or Genetic Variable?	115

11 Implications 117

11.1	The Registrar-General's Class Scheme	118
11.2	Justifications of the use of the Social Class Scheme for Women	119
11.3	Other Possible Schema	121
11.4	Desiderata for a Classification	124
11.5	A Tall Story	126
11.6	Implications for Theory and Empirical Research	127
11.7	Describing and Explaining Inequalities	130

References   132

Name Index   137

Subject Index   139

List of Tables

2.1	Stevenson's 'validation' of the SCS	16
3.1	Distribution per 1000 of economically active and retired males by their own social class, 1931, 1951 and 1971 (England and Wales)	26
3.2	Census: recoded sample of employed men, 1970 and 1980 classifications (England and Wales)	29
4.1	Women's relationship to head of household	37
4.2	Marital status of women and their relationship to the head of household	38
4.3	Women's social class according to different assignment rules	39
5.1	Goodness-of-fit statistics for different models testing homogamy hypotheses	47
5.1(a)	Three-way cross-tabulation of husband, wife and wife's father's occupation, 1956–60	48
5.1(b)	Three-way cross-tabulation of husband, wife and wife's father's occupation, 1966–70	50
5.1(c)	Three-way cross-tabulation of husband, wife and wife's father's occupation, 1976–80	51
6.1	Age at first birth by pure husband's social class by woman's own height	65
6.2	Percentage of prematurity broken down by mothers' height and by husbands' social class, 1976–80	65
8.1	Percentage reporting excellent or good health	77
8.2	Reported disability (the GHS question) broken down by test indices	78
8.3	Percentage of population giving positive Nottingham Health Project (NHP) score	78

List of Tables ix

8.4	Percentage of pre-eclampsia broken down by mother's height and by husband's social class, 1976–80	79
8.5	Percentage of premature births in Aberdeen, 1976–80, according to test indices	80
8.6	Proportion of population giving positive GHQ score	81
8.7	Mean number of reported psycho-social symptoms	81
8.8	Percentage leaving school with no further qualifications by height and HORG	82
8.9	Rateable value in 1981 (£) in Aberdeen by test indices of measures of female social class	83
8.10	Percentage owner-occupiers (%)	84
8.11	Mean number of consumer durables by height and by husband's social class	84
8.12	Smokes now (%)	85
8.13	Slimming (%)	85
8.14	Drinks less than once a week (%)	86
8.15	Percentage of teenage first births in Aberdeen, 1976–80, according to test indices	87
8.16	Percentage of pre-nuptial conceptions in Aberdeen, 1976–80, according to test indices	87
8.17	Percentage of low birthweight in Aberdeen, 1976–80, by test indices	88
8.18	Average IQ according to husband's social class and mother's height (in four categories)	89
8.19	Interviewer's assessment of the mother (vocabulary, fluency and logical thought)	90
8.20	Percentage of pre-eclampsia according to husband's social class in three periods	91
8.21	Percentage of pre-eclampsia according to mother's height in three periods	91
8.22	Percentage of premature births according to husband's social class in three periods	92

List of Tables

8.23	Percentage of premature births broken down by mother's height in three periods	93
8.24	Percentage of women who smoke according to husband's social class in three periods	93
8.25	Percentage of women who smoke broken down by mother's height in three periods	94
8.26	Percentage of pre-nuptial conceptions according to husband's social class in three periods	95
8.27	Percentage of pre-nuptial conceptions according to mother's height in three periods	95
8.28	Percentage of low birthweight according to husband's social class in three periods	96
8.29	Percentage of low birthweight according to mother's height in three periods	96
9.1	Reported disability (the GHS question) according to height	102
9.2	Percentage restricted activity by various height measures	102
9.3	Drinks less than once a week (%)	103
9.4	Smokes now	103
9.5	Percentage reporting slimming during last year	104
9.6	Percentage energetic by various height measures	104
9.7	Whether or not owner-occupier (%)	105
9.8	Height compatibility among spouses	106
10.1	Child malnutrition and other developmental indicators in seven African countries around 1980	110
10.2	Mean heights among young adults (20–24) and difference between social class I and II and IV and V since 1940	111
10.3	Difference in height and self-reported health measures between social classes in age groups	112
10.3A	Standard errors of difference	112
10.4	West of Scotland Twenty 07 Study	112
10.5	Mean height of women by husband's and father's occupational classes	114

Preface

What is social class? Do we all have one? Does it matter? Arguing about the nature of a classification into social class provides endless hours of fun for social scientists, and – not to be sneezed at – subject matter for student assignments. But there is a serious issue underlying the academic ping-pong. What kind of society do we live in? Is it one where our life chances are dominated by the long shadows cast by our family bakcground, by a relatively enduring social structure, or are there many opportunities for social advancement, even for the circulation of elites?

Such questions are usually asked about men, and argument about the nature of the classification 'therefore' revolve around the salience of current occupation – the basis for an assignment to a social class – to male life chances. If women are considered at all, it is usually as an appendages to their husbands or, if they have been careless and either lost or not found one, to their fathers. It would be astonishing if (female) social scientists did not complain. They do.

The argument, however, tends to get 'stuck' there. It is clear that women object to being 'tacked on' to their (possibly non-existent) husbands but, when a substantial minority of women have never had a *paid* job, there is no obvious way of assigning them to a social class on an occupational basis. Proposals to change the whole basis are rare, and existing schema defended along the lines of not throwing out the baby with the bath water.

That may be fine in an academic journal, but it will not do when confronted with data. The poor unfortunates like ourselves are left to soldier on with a totally inadequate instrument. In our particular case, we were concerned to understand the patterns of pregnancy-related outcomes in a large data base spanning 30 years – the Aberdeen Maternity and Neo Natal Bank (see Samphier and Thompson, 1982, for a full description). There were clearly variations captured by the occupationally based measures available to us and hence substantial inequality in pregnancy outcomes. But further analysis led us to an interpretative quagmire. This book explains our frustration and what we did about it.

We see this as a general problem for those concerned to analyse patterns of social inequality which is particularly acute when considering inequalities between women who are included only as an afterthought in available classification systems. We think that our method of approaching the problem of describing, measuring and hopefully understanding patterns of inequality

– especially between women – should be adopted more often. Data should be respected, not forced into a classification.

This is therefore a methodological study of occupationally-based social class classifications. It is not a theoretical book about class, although the theories underlying any appeal to class structure to justify the use of the social class scheme in various ways are considered where appropriate; and the applicability of class theory to the position of women is of particular interest. Equally, it is not a methods book delving into the intricacies of occupation coding, although we make some pertinent remarks about those who continue to tinker, apparently theoretically, with the existing occupational classifications. Instead, the book addresses the problem of what is it we are trying to do when we classify an individual, and particularly a women, into a social class grouping and how this classification illuminates, or obscures, in any given context.

The methodological focus means that the book will be of interest to all kinds of social and behavioural scientists, including educationalists, medical sociologists, epidemiologists, political scientists, social historians, social policy analysts, and statisticians. It should also be of interest to those bureaucrats, both national and international, who insist on spending large quantities of time and effort on tinkering with the occupational classification.

ROY A. CARR-HILL
COLIN W. PRITCHARD

Acknowledgements

We are grateful to the Medical Research Council (MRC) and to the guardians of the Aberdeen Maternity and Neo-Natal Data Bank (AMNDB) for providing us with access to the data which formed the basis of the argument. Equally, we are indebted to Raymond Illsley, whose original article in 1955 provided the windmill against which to tilt our statistical lances; it was the giant.

Our own analysis has evolved over nearly a decade and, at different stages, parts of the arguments have been presented to seminars at the MRC Medical Sociology Unit at Aberdeen in 1982, the Scottish Medical Sociology Group in Dundee in 1982, the Equal Opportunities Commission Workshop on Female Social Class at Guildford in 1983, the staff/postgraduate Sociology Seminar at the University of York in 1984, the staff/post-graduate Sociology Seminar at the University of Essex in 1985 and the Department of Community Medicine and Epidemiology in Nottingham in 1987. We are grateful to the respective audiences for their patience and their suggestions. We have also inflicted the manuscript in whole or in parts upon Pamela Gillies, Sally Macintyre and Rory Williams, and we are very grateful for their comments. The responsibility for the *oeuvre*, of course, remains ours.

We would also like to express our gratitude to the assistance we have received from Vanessa Windass, who has organised all the word processing, from James Bowen and Jenny Hardy, who between them have organised the indices, and from Simon Baldwin and Keith Humphreys, who have extracted sundry tables where required. Finally Roy Carr-Hill acknowledges the support of the Economic and Social Research Council's grant to the Centre for Health Economics and Colin Pritchard the support of the Scottish Home and Health Department's grant to the Social Paediatric and Obstetric Research Unit whilst completing the book; and both of us would like to thank our households for their support.

ROY A. CARR-HILL
COLIN W. PRITCHARD

1 Introduction

The focus of our study is an empirical problem: how do we classify women in terms of social position in a way which will be consistent and illuminating? For us, the problem arose because of our specific professional interest in analysing patterns of pregnancy-related outcomes among women in a large data base spanning 30 years; but the problem is general when examining variations among women because the classic solution is not very useful and is unacceptable to many.

Our database included a range of occupational data both about the women's own occupations and those of their fathers and husbands. In accordance with venerable tradition, the occupational data had been classified in terms of the Registrar-General's Social Class Scheme (or SCS). In common with many researchers before us, we found ourselves faced with a whole series of conceptual and empirical problems when using the classification, eventually convincing ourselves that a better understanding of the basis and detailed working of the Scheme would allow us to derive clearer and more analytically tractable tools. At a distance of some years, this was a foolishly naive hope. However, we have learnt a lot from the endeavour. This book sets out to share our experience and, we think, contribute to a greater understanding of the issues involved.

Although our interest in the problem grew out of this very specific context, we would argue that it is a *general* difficulty with analysing variations in the condition and situation of women. For example, in an otherwise crystal-clear exposition of *Social Class Differences in Britain*, Reid (1981) must mystify many a student with the commentary on his Table 3.1 (p. 71), showing the distribution of men and women by social class, when he says: 'When looking at the sex differences here, it should be borne in mind that it is normally the male occupation which provides the basis of social class allocation' (pp. 70–1).

Indeed, although our discussion and empirical analysis of the occupational classification – in Parts 2 and 3 – starts with birth-related outcomes, our concern is with variation in a wide range of conditions, processes and situations. Furthermore we believe that our argument – in directing attention to the kinds of criteria upon which a classification should be based – is also relevant to the issue of how best to represent social position both for men and women.

1.1 THE RELEVANCE OF DEBATES ABOUT CLASS

While we argue that the problem addressed in this book is more general than the specific circumstances in which the problem arose for us, we need to make it clear that this is not a typical book about 'social class' or even a typical contribution to the growing literature on 'women and social class'. In the first place, the starting point is not a theoretical stance deriving from any variant of 'class theory': the problem which we are addressing (one which is shared with many others) is how to understand empirical variation.

This does not mean that our approach is atheoretical; on the contrary, our examination of the data has posed us with a series of theoretical problems about how the social class classification arose, why it has taken this particular form, how it is used and how it works. The basic criteria which we apply to the theoretical debate are, however, a little unusual, relating to the consistency and empirical usefulness of the formulations they imply rather than to the internal logic of the theories. Of course, in an ideal world, theory sets the framework for empirical observation and empirical observation would guide the development of theory. However, the data are never sufficient to reflect the complexities and subtleties required by any of the theoretical formulations and one is often forced to work with whatever the available classification measures are, rather than with some ideal index derived from theoretical precepts.

This measurement problem is, of course, ubiquitous, especially with official data; class is no exception. Hindness (1973) may argue that the social class classification can be related to Marxist categories, but that only shifts rather than solves the problem. In the case of men, most authors struggle on through the multiple layers of reflection and reification. All too often the results are curious if used to comment on theory, as the result may well have arisen from the inappropriate application of the social class classification. The analysis of the origins of social class in Chapters 2 and 3 illustrates the dangers. In the case of women, the problem is compounded: indeed, many argue that the social class classification is so flawed as to be essentially irrelevant (Oakley, 1981). But whilst we sympathise with that position (see below, Chapters 4 and 11), this does not solve our problem when faced with a set of useful empirical data where the social class classification has been deployed. It is, therefore, essential to understand *theoretically* the relation between data and the 'reality' they are supposed to reflect.

Second, we shall not, in the body of the book, dwell on the theoretical argument about the nature of female social class. This does not mean we would deny its importance; in fact, we would suggest that the argument in this book is very relevant to that theoretical debate because, whilst the classification of women has indeed been 'tacked on' to the original (male) social class scheme so that the theoretical critique is well founded, its proponents have tended to ignore many of the lessons that might be learnt from data.

There is, of course, a growing strand in the contemporary debate about female social class which focuses on what is an appropriate empirical classification of households. These are considered at the appropriate points of Chapters 4, 5 and 11; here we describe briefly the theoretical debate about the treatment of women in the social class scheme as part of the context for the argument of this book.

1.2 CONVENTIONAL TREATMENTS OF WOMEN IN THE CLASS DEBATE

On the face of it class theory, be it Marxist, British neo-Weberian or functionalist, provides some sort of justification for the social class scheme and its treatment of women. They are united at least to the extent that they adopt a common 'conventional' view. The central tenet of this view is that stratification theory is about the explanation of class inequalities: that is, inequalities that arise out of the economic and occupational structure of societies. Both class theory and the SCS are grounded in occupation and provide maps of the occupational structure.

The conventional view goes further than that, however. We will show that the official practice of classifying women according to the occupational class of the men with whom they live, arose almost casually out of the inherent assumption that women shared their class with the families in which they live. The theoretical assumption underpinning this position is, however, far from casual. As Abbott and Sapsford (1987) pointed out, the notion that women derive their class position from the men with whom they live implies: 'a theoretical statement that women's experiences, loyalties and social action are not their own in the sense that men's are' (p. 2).

Thus, according to functionalist accounts, the crucial function of the family is to fulfil society's 'need' to reproduce itself, both by providing new members to replace those who die and by socialising those new members. The family 'system' is articulated with the economic 'system' through the individual who holds the dual family and economic roles: typically the male 'head' of the household who provides 'instrumental leadership' for the family (compare Parsons, 1956, p. 13 *et seq.*). The functionalist account of the family has been subjected to detailed critique over the years, specifically in terms of its evasion of gender inequality.

The 'natural' opposite to the 'functionalist' perspective is class theory, where status is a subjective evaluation arising historically from patterns of inequality in economic position and power. Such an analysis, on the face of it, also seems to exclude gender inequality. Many class theorists do, of course, recognise gender inequality; but they argue that 'class' is the key to understanding the nature of stratification and that class is in general about the social division of labour, and in particular that the occupational structure (which is one way of describing the economic system) provides a convenient set of descriptions for that social division.

More recently, the 'conventional view' has been defended on the grounds that it is empirically the case that, for by far the majority of conjugal families, the man is: 'the family member who has the greatest commitment to, and continuity in, labour market participation' (Goldthorpe, 1983, p. 470). This less ideal-typical view provides a counter to the difficulties that arise with the simple conventional view when the participation of women in the labour force has increased. Thus Goldthorpe acknowledges that dual-earner families might pose a problem but argues that patterns of married women's employment are determined by the (male) class structure. The current concern with: ' "cross-class" families ... [should] ... be regarded far more as artefacts of an inappropriate mode of categorisation than as a quantitatively significant feature of present-day society. Rather than marriage being the source of new complexity in the class structure, it would seem that class still remains the basis of homogamy' (p. 482).

In reply to his critics (Heath and Britten, 1984; Stanworth, 1984) who seek to show that women's jobs do make a difference to political behaviour and that the class experience of wives differs from that of their husbands, Goldthorpe (1984) replies that: 'From the standpoint of class analysis, how far variation in any particular aspect of social behaviour or relationships ... can actually be accounted for in terms of class membership is entirely a matter for investigation' (p. 491).

Goldthorpe, then, is arguing for a particular definition of class and is engaged in the project of discovering the extent to which 'social behaviour or relationships' can be accounted for in those terms. He does allow empirical data a role, but only to confirm whether or not women fit into his class system. This is rather a long way from the project of analysing inequalities between women.

It might be that this is the end point of this argument: we can and should dispense with the notion of class *qua* occupational position in considering inequalities between women. After all, we are repeatedly told by the most

Introduction 5

reputable class theorists that 'women are peripheral to the class system' (Parkin, 1979, pp. 14–15). From the women's point of view, the class system is peripheral to them; or, as Delphy (1977) succinctly puts it, a woman's 'standard of living does not depend on her class relationship to the proletariat, but on her serf relations of production with her husband' (p. 19).

The failure of class theory to incorporate women and its dominance in the study of stratification has led to a strong feminist critique of stratification theory itself. As Dex (1985) points out, the attack is not on any particular theory of stratification but on all major theories. On the positive side, feminist theorists have attempted to revise class theory to take account of women's class relationships and, more fundamentally, to generate a new account of stratification theory as a whole. The details of the contemporary theoretical debate within a broadly feminist perspective are concisely reviewed by Abbott and Sapsford (1987, pp. 4–11). As they conclude: 'the debate concerning the incorporation of women into stratification theory is a complex one at this level, and different "schools" take different lines on how it should be achieved' (pp. 10–11).

The debate, both as a general set-to between feminism and class analysis and within feminist theory itself, remains unresolved. There are some recent attempts to provide classificatory schema that represent women more appropriately. These are considered in more detail in the concluding chapter, but they are fraught with difficulties. Important though the theoretical project is, the immediate problem is an empirical one when faced with large volumes of data which require classification prior to analysis.

1.3 THE STRUCTURE OF THE BOOK

The ground clearing exercise carried out above suggests the importance of understanding the genesis and origins of the existing social classification of women, and this is the purpose of the first part of the book (Chapters 2, 3, 4 and 5). We argue that the classification of women cannot be understood without an understanding of the origins of the social class classification itself; and so, in Chapter 2, we review the genesis of the Registrar-General's SCS. We emphasise that Stevenson was concerned to develop a classification to answer a particular problem and we conclude with Szreter (1984) that 'Stevenson became firmly wedded to his alternative explanatory theory which was premised on the hereditarian naturalistic model of social structure' (p. 538). In Chapter 3 we show how, despite multifarious tinkerings over the last 50 years, Stevenson's classification is still the basis of the SCS we use today.

In Chapter 4 we turn to the place of women in the scheme. We show how Stevenson justified ignoring women in the classification he developed and how the contemporary use of husband's social class depends on the presumption of class homogamy. Chapter 5 therefore examines data available to us from the Aberdeen Maternity and Neo Natal Data Bank which suggests that the case for presuming homogamy is weak. The only remaining justification for using husband's social class to represent the status of their unfortunate spouses is that, in practice, as an index, it works.

However, a pragmatic claim of that nature has to be assessed empirically relative to other possible indices. This is the focus of the second part. In Chapter 6 we discuss the criteria for a 'good' and 'useful' classification in this sense. We argue that an index should not, in general, of itself explain; that is should provide a relatively sensitive and unique assignment to a category; that it should be derived from easily collectable data; and, preferably, that it should be ordinal. On those criteria, social class is a loser. We then consider, as did Stevenson, our specific problem and, after describing the various options that were available to us, suggest that the woman's own height is, *at least in terms of the criteria*, a not implausible candidate.

Nevertheless, that is only half of the pragmatic problem of assessing the utility of a classification. We also have to specify the range of phenomena over which we expect the index to be useful. This is the focus of Chapter 7. Typically the social class classification is deployed for men as being relevant to all (socially) valued outcomes, and so the issue is what counts as the appropriate 'test' set of socially valued outcomes. Drawing on work in the area of quality of life measurement we outline a wide range of phenomena to which such an index should be relevant. At the same time, we are constrained by the data we could lay our hands on, and sources we propose to tap are indicated at the appropriate places.

The final chapter in this sequence (Chapter 8) compares the discriminatory power of the social class classification derived from the husband's occupation (henceforth HORG: based on husbands' occupation as categorised by the Registrar-General) with that of a woman's own height. We show that, whilst HORG is sometimes spectacularly good at discriminating outcomes, it is erratic and that this is especially a problem with those unassigned to a social class classification. Women's height, whilst statistically less powerful, is more consistent.

Up to this point, the empirical argument concentrates on the power of HORG or the woman's own height to display variation. In the third part of the book, we ask what role is height playing. First, in Chapter 9, we return to the problem of class endogamy which was a crucial plank in our argument against HORG in Chapter 5, and ask whether a husband's height could be used as a convenient discriminator for his spouse's life chances, just as HORG is presently used as a 'better' measure than women's own occupation. Second, we explore the empirical properties of the discrimination afforded by height in Chapter 10. We show how the height variable can be used as an indicator of poor (physical) development and we repeat Illsley's (1955) analysis to show that height still accounts for some of intergenerational female social mobility.

The final chapter of the book draws the lessons from all this, We emphasise the importance of an empirical examination in assessing the value of any index, and we conclude by assessing the implications of this analysis for the debate about the nature of female social class.

Part I
The Genesis of the Current Social Classification of Women

2 The Registrar-General's Social Class Scheme: The Stevenson Version

2.1 INTRODUCTION

The Registrar-General's SCS provides by far the most common social classification used in Britain by sociologists, epidemiologists and official statisticians. The reporting of social class information is almost routine, while the use of the highly derivative Market Research Classification dominates commercial surveys.

The present SCS is based on occupation. It involves the collection of a set of occupational data and the use of a cumbersome series of rules to assign individuals into social classes. For women, the procedure is further complicated, first by the predominant practice of assigning them to a social class based on their husband's occupation, and second because not all women have husbands.

Our problem is to assess the extent to which husband's occupation classified according to the Registrar-General's SCS is a useful instrument for classifying women. In the first instance, this depends on understanding the SCS itself. Given that this Scheme has been elaborated in various ways over the century and frequently refined for different purposes, it is important to explore its genesis in order to understand the import of later modifications and its application to women.

However, the origins of the SCS and the processes which have led to its subsequent modification in general, and in particular for women, are far from clear. The most recently available semi-official account of the origins of SCS is that provided by Leete and Fox (1977). Their account, however, is simply too brief and lacking in detail to contribute substantially to an understanding of the current SCS.

The purpose of this chapter is to examine the circumstances surrounding its inception in rather more detail. The impact of subsequent modifications is examined in Chapter 3 and the incorporation of women into the Scheme is discussed in Chapter 4.

2.2 ORIGINS OF THE SOCIAL CLASS SCHEME ACCORDING TO STEVENSON

The SCS was first used in the Registrar-General's Decennial Report for 1911 (published by the General Registry Office in 1913). Dr Stevenson, who was the superintendent of statistics at the General Registry Office (GRO), based his scheme on the material collected through the Census and Vital Registration systems which had been evolved during the nineteenth century.

Data on occupations had been originally collected primarily to describe economic activity and, since 1851, the basic distinctions were in terms of the materials worked on (for example, occupations in the iron industry or in the textile industry). The realisation that one could be, for example, a 'clerk' almost anywhere led to the proliferation of occupational titles (such as clerk in the iron industry, or clerk in the textile industry). This uneasy mixture was not *a priori* suitable for a coherent social classification as Stevenson commented:

> it is by no means precise, for in many cases, especially in commerce and industry, the census occupational description gives no indication of social position. The farmer, for instance, may farm 10 acres or 1,000, and the draper may own the establishment or be his lowest paid assistant or labourer. As a result, many men, especially business men, belonging to the middle-classes have necessarily been included with the working class. (p. xli)

Stevenson, however, felt he had little choice but to use these data. He developed the SCS primarily for the analysis of fertility and infant mortality. Actuarial work in the previous century (for example, Ansell, 1874) had shown marked discrepancies in mortality in the first five years of life between the different strata of society (the contemporary importance of class patterns of fertility is discussed later). For the first time, in 1911, births were enumerated according to occupation groups which made possible the calculation of rates of fertility and of infant mortality (per 1000 live births) on an occupational basis. For legitimate births, occupation-specific rates were calculated on the basis of the husband's occupation, while the mother's own occupation was used for illegitimate births.

Stevenson recognised from the beginning that the 'occupational' classification available which provided the building blocks for SCS was far from satisfactory for his purposes. The Census Report for 1911 notes:

Both personal and industrial classifications of occupations have their particular uses, the former being useful especially in connection with questions of vital statistics, the latter in connection with questions of economics. The classification which has been evolved in this country combines both of these objects but fulfils neither of them completely. (p. viii)

For the Census of 1911 a concerted attempt was made to separate personal and industrial classifications of occupations, the intention being to cross-classify them and to generate a basic classification which could be grouped by personal occupation or by industry according to the needs of the analysis. The experiment was regarded as a failure, principally on the grounds that the occupational classification suffered from problems of inadequate description in the Census returns. The conclusion was: 'As a result of the experience so gained we have reluctantly come to the conclusions that ... any logically consistent tabulation in our Census of workers by personal occupation is unattainable and that the present system of classification, partly by occupation and partly by product, must be adhered to' (pp. vii–ix). The basic data available to Stevenson from the 1911 Census were, then, far from apt for his purposes. Nevertheless he felt it possible to produce an approximate social grading of occupations.

The Report explains the form of the classification: five hierarchically ordered classes and three additional classes for particular industries. The five ranked classes were based on tripartite division: the 'upper and middle' non-manual class (Class 1); skilled workmen (Class 3); and the unskilled workmen (Class 5). Classes 2 and 4 were intermediate classes, consisting of those 'industrial' occupations which were believed to contain unknown mixture of non-manual and skilled manual workers in the case of Class 2, for example. The underlying criteria by which the occupations were grouped are not clear; indeed, the Report itself notes the difficulties with the industrial basis of the occupational classification, which meant that the assignment of occupations into social groups was 'by no means precise'.

The essential features of the classification of 1911 are fairly similar to those of the present SCS. It was based on some intuitive notion of social rank. The crucial features which determined the grouping occupations were the division between manual and non-manual occupations and the distinction between skilled and unskilled manual occupations. Although the logic of using male occupations as the basis for the analysis of legitimate births is not spelt out, the registration procedures left little alternative; and the belief that the social status of members of the same family were similar/identical

Stevenson's Version of Social Class Scheme 13

seems to have been regarded as axiomatic. The use of the SCS for 1911 data to analyse fertility and infant mortality makes it clear that occupation was seen as an indicator of the family's probable social position rather than of intrinsic interest.

What mostly concerned Stevenson, however, were the problems associated with the occupational classification itself. Referring to the changes in the classification introduced in 1921, he commented (1923):

> Social status can broadly be deduced from a genuine occupational classification, but not from an industrial, where all grades of worker, master and man, skilled and unskilled, are grouped together for each industry ... Much better results should be attainable for the future if a determined effort was made to purge the classification of its industrial taint in 1921, accompanied by the introduction of an entirely independent industrial classification. (p. 328)

The classification of occupations in 1921 was seen as a radical overhaul. Its introduction, with its separate occupational and industrial classifications, followed a report of a joint committee from social government departments.[1] The logic of the 'new' SCS is best explained in Stevenson's paper to the Royal Statistical Society in February 1928 and it is worth following the argument of that paper in some detail.

Stevenson's intention was to justify the choice of occupation from amongst the data available in the Census and Vital Registration; this choice was not axiomatic for him. His paper starts with a brief review of attempts to compare the vital statistics of more or less prosperous sections of the community. Looking at the data available from the Census and Vital Registration systems he rejects the use of both geographical and household variables. Geographical variations, he argues, are difficult to interpret because the mixture of poverty and wealth in particular areas is impossible to determine. He goes on to say: 'The ideal method would classify individuals, not whole populations, by their degree of prosperity' (p. 207). The use of household data, such as the number of rooms relative to the number of occupants, is also rejected.[2] Here he argues that the classification would capture two possible factors which may contribute to mortality: 'In examining returns compiled on this basis it would be impossible to say how far the mortality excess of the two- over the four-room class was due to poverty and how far to overcrowding' (p. 208). The argument here is that, to be useful, an indicator of relative prosperity or poverty ought not, of itself, to have direct effects on the outcome considered.

So far, Stevenson has argued as if what he sought was an indicator of relative wealth. However, he next turns his attention to what the underlying concept of the social grading ought to be. He notes that mortality statistics based on family income had recently been compiled in the United States. However, he doubts the value of the use of income data, even if it were routinely collected in Britain:[3]

> But its drawback is that it may fail altogether as an index of culture, probably the more important influence. The power of culture to exert a favourable influence upon mortality, even in the complete absence of wealth, is well illustrated in the case of the clergy. The income test, if it could be applied, would certainly place them well down the list, yet their mortality is remarkably low. (p. 209)

Stevenson goes on to argue that this aspect, 'culture',

> is more easily estimated as between occupations than wealth, so the occupational basis of social grading has a wholesome tendency to emphasise it. One does not hesitate to allocate the clergy, despite their unfortunately all too frequent poverty, to the highest social class, and similarly, in other cases, regard can be paid, not only to probable income, but to cultured intelligence and education. (p. 209)

The basis of the social position which Stevenson hoped to define, then, is what he calls 'culture' which, although it may tend to be associated with prosperity, is not exclusively so. The classification remains essentially intuitive: Stevenson and his audience recognised the absurdity of a classification that would place publicans 'above' clergymen.[4]

Allowing that it would be possible to rank occupations according to the 'culture' of the individuals engaged in them, the problem of how to combine the different occupations so as to derive fairly large groups which are roughly homogeneous in terms of social position (considered as relative 'culture') remains. Stevenson explains his resolution to the problem as follows:

> But all we need to know for the purposes of the distinction sought is that certain groups of occupations are associated with culture and (in the higher grades) open to the opportunities of certain sections of society and not others. The son of a carpenter may not follow in his father's occupational footsteps, but is at least likely to become an artisan of some sort. Hence, if the occupational groupings are kept wide enough, their association with social gradation may be expected to be close. Such speculation, however, must be submitted to the test of experience. (pp. 210–11)

The idea seems to be that, allied to a reasonably stable occupational structure, there is a reasonably stable opportunity structure. Although that opportunity structure does not determine the actual job someone will do, it tends to determine the sorts of job open to people with certain sorts of background. The sorts of occupation open to people with certain sorts of background, Stevenson suggests, fall together into groups which are roughly homogenous in terms of 'culture'. Stevenson does point out that the task would be simplified if there were a caste structure. The actual class boundaries which Stevenson drew were certainly not derived from a detailed empirical study of the occupations of fathers and sons; the basis is, once again, intuitive.

The form of the final 1921 classification is, in fact, similar to that derived for 1911. It is based on the tripartite division of non-manual, skilled manual and unskilled manual with intermediate classes for doubtful cases:

> Classes 1, 3 and 5 are clearly defined so far as the occupations actually assigned to them are concerned, for the classification implies that all doubtful cases are assigned to classes 2 and 4 ... Of course, there must be many men included in 2 and 4 who might appropriately be assigned to the class above or below if all the facts were known and they could be dealt with as individuals, but in this case the occupations have to be dealt with as a whole, and no fact relevant to the social position of the individual except his occupation can be taken into account. (p. 212)

The social classes are groupings of occupations, not of individuals. No account is taken of the high-earning, cultured artisan as an individual, although the perceived probability of finding such individuals within an occupation is taken into account by the possibility of assigning the occupation to an intermediate class.

Stevenson goes on to say:

> The scheme is admittedly a rough-and-ready one, as indeed all broad lines of classification devoid of quantitive basis must be, but it has the great merit of simplicity, and the results of its application, which are published in the recently issued report on occupational vital statistics seem to me to point to its fundamental soundness. (p. 212)

The apparently circular nature of Stevenson's argument for the soundness of his scheme *in practice* is considered in section 2.4 below:[5] here we continue with the attempt to understand what he thought he was doing. The evidence that Stevenson adduces for the fundamental soundness of the classification is the evidence of fertility and mortality gradients. He demonstrates rising fertility and mortality with descending social class (see Table 2.1).

The underlying concept of social organisation to which Stevenson seems to be referring is one of a relatively stable and rigid hierarchy, differentiated by 'culture'. The actual meaning of 'culture' in Stevenson's sense is far from clear: it is closely associated with prosperity, or at least with some freedom from the pressing necessities of penury (the 'comfortable classes' are also the cultured classes). But it is also an attempt to express the intuitive sense that a simple measurement of wealth would not place, for example, clergy and publicans 'correctly' in the social order. It would be convenient to feel that Professor Greenwood, in his contemporary comment on Stevenson's paper (Stevenson, 1928, p. 221), had presented a complete picture in his summation: 'I think Dr. Stevenson means by "wealth" the purchasing power of the family unit, and by "culture", not an acquaintance with differential equations or the minor poems of Horace, but a combination of knowledge and skill which enables a person to use his purchasing power wisely (p. 221). Certainly, the 'wise' use of purchasing power would be an attribute of the cultured (in Stevenson's sense) individual.[6] However, Stevenson's notion of culture would seem to incorporate a more general view of 'cultured intelligence and education', which would distinguish peasant frugality from the prosperous individual's investment in things of 'lasting worth'.

In using occupation as an indicator of social position Stevenson seems to have paid attention to both 'probable income' and to 'culture'. The

Table 2.1 Stevenson's 'validation' of the SCS

	Natality*	Mortality†	Infant mortality‡
Class I	70	81	48
Class II	74	94	70
Class III	107	95	97
Class IV	116	101	113
Class V	127	126	123

* Birth rate per 1000 married males under 50 (1921).
† Crude death rate (1921–3).
‡ Death rate under 1 year old (1921–3).
Source: Stevenson (1928).

classification is not, however, based on any empirical knowledge about incomes (or likely income) or any attempt to operationalise the concept of culture. It would, of course, be unfair to criticise Stevenson for failing to do what he could not do, given his position. Nevertheless, the point is that the basis for the grouping of occupations into social classes is not empirical and does not derive from any articulate or coherent social theory; it is fundamentally an intuitive grouping based on the experience of living in a particular sector of the society it was intended to classify.

In some ways, of course, Stevenson had little choice: the occupational data were unique among routinely collected official statistics in that they permitted broad inferences to be drawn about relative prosperity and culture through an appeal to a common understanding of the nature of society. But, overall, this review supports the impression Leete and Fox (1977) give of a progression from a need to know about mortality rates in different strata of society to the fully-fledged scheme used in the analyses of the 1921 data. However, questions of why the classification took the form it did, both in general and in detail, remain unanswered.

2.3 THE IDEOLOGICAL CONTEXT OF A SOCIAL CLASSIFICATION: SZRETER

Szreter (1984) has convincingly suggested that the eventual form of the SCS can best be understood in terms of Stevenson's attempts to address issues of contemporary political and academic concern. His argument starts with the puzzle of why, given the need for information expressed by Humphreys (then Assistant Registrar-General) in 1887, it took until 1913 to produce the required system of classification.

The failure of the 1911 attempt to separate a personal and industrial classification meant that Stevenson used essentially the same occupational classification as in 1891; the practical and conceptual apparatus for conducting such an analysis was already available. Thus occupation-specific mortality figures had been routinely reported in Decennial Supplements from 1851–2 onwards; actuarial work, such as life tables produced by Ansell (1874) for the 'upper' and 'middle' classes, had demonstrated the importance of socially differentiated childhood mortality;[7] and Humphreys had drawn on a 'class' analysis by Grimshaw (1877, he was the Registrar-General for Ireland) in making his argument.

Such an analysis, on the face of it, would have served the promotion of schemes of public sanitation, a 'political' aim which had long been part of the tradition of the GRO. If the progression had been as straightforward as

Leete and Fox (1977) imply, there seems no reason why the analysis was not attempted using the data collected in 1891 or, at least, in 1901. Szreter argues that the reasons behind the quarter of a century delay in the introduction of 'class' analysis lie in the contemporary debate between the environmentalist conception of 'class' and 'those who believed that the social structure more or less reflected a natural hierarchy of ability and mortality in society' (Szreter, 1984, p. 526). If the concept of 'class' was successfully appropriated by those who saw it as a 'natural hierarchy', the environmentalist policies of intervention, principally by works of public santitation, would have been undermined. Indeed, proponents of the 'hereditarian' view of social structure regarded interventions to improve the lot of disadvantaged sections of the community as positively harmful. Szreter suggests that the 1891 commissioning of William Ogle's special investigation into local variations in infant mortality (1892) and Dunbar's (1907) detailed analysis of survivorship rates in selected localities were returns to the sure ground of the environmentalist argument in the face of the hereditarian interpretations based on 'class'.[8]

Shortly after the turn of the century, the debate between environmentalist and hereditarian views was to become more politically and emotionally charged by the discussion surrounding the report of the Interdepartmental Inquiry on Physical Degeneration, which had been set up primarily in response to the poor physical condition of recruits for the Boer Wars. From the environmentalist point of view, the poor physical condition stood as an indictment of the living conditions of large sections of the community. From the hereditarian stance, it was evidence that the 'national stock' was deteriorating because of the differential fertility of the higher and lower classes.

Szreter (1984) notes the minutes of the GRO committee on the Census early in 1910 where it was recorded that: 'Dr Stevenson was rather anxious if possible to get fertility coefficients for 3 grades of society. The upper and middle classes, he said were constantly being accused of not reproducing themselves and he thought it desirable that statistics should verify or deny this accusation' (Public Record Office, RG 19/48B, p. 62). In this light, the SCS of 1913 can be seen as addressing a central issue in the theoretical and practical debate surrounding the quest for 'national reproductive efficiency' in maintaining the 'national stock'.

If the general intentions of the SCS can be seen in terms of the contemporary debate, the form which the classification took was also influenced by the terms of the debate. In general, 'class' was seen in roughly occupational terms long before (for example, Smith, 1793, reprinted in 1970) the particular controversy between the environmentalist and hereditarian views arose.

However, the hereditarian point of view postulated a distribution of mental and physical abilities which were more or less directly reflected in the level of intellectual or manual skill implied in an occupation. Although physical and mental abilities were thought of as being related, intellectual ability was, axiomatically, thought of as being of a higher order than physical attributes. The hierarchy from non-manual to skilled manual to unskilled manual could be interpreted as a direct reflection of hierarchy of 'genetic worth'.

The fact that Stevenson's SCS resembles that promulgated by hereditarian theorists does not necessarily imply that he embraced their theoretical perspective. Thus Szreter (1984) suggests that Stevenson's work 'should be seen as conducting an open scientific debate with the strong claims of this *a priori* position ... Eugenicist language and concepts permeated his work because they were the principal antagonists in a debate which Stevenson had deliberately entered into' (p. 527).

The particular hierarchical arrangement of the classes in the SCS of 1913 was a direct consequence of the terms of that debate. Tellingly, Szreter (1984, pp. 533–4) argues that the three additional classes for certain large occupations acknowledged the special environmental, social and occupational characteristics long known to be associated with those occupations. Their inclusion in the main scheme would have led to a particular contamination of the test for the correlates of 'social position'.

However, the general intention appears to have changed between the Censuses of 1911 and 1921. The testing of the competing hypotheses in the debate about national efficiency had implied an interest in both inter- and intra-class differentials in fertility and mortality (*vide* Stevenson, 1920 and 1923). In fact the raw data on differential fertility and mortality supported the hereditarian view (see Table 2.1), and Stevenson set about accounting for these differentials in other terms. In any case, by the time of his paper in 1928, Stevenson was convinced, first of the primacy of interclass differences and second of the adequacy of the SCS. Szreter (1984) sums up Stevenson's intellectual journey as follows:

> Thus, it was in order to counter, or at least to test, the claims being made by hereditarian 'sociologists' at the beginning of the century that Stevenson had originally adopted their morally evaluative view of society as a unidimensionally graded hierarchy of occupations. His subsequent analysis conclusively proved wrong both variants of a hereditarian interpretation of the fertility decline, as a fecundity deterioration. But, through this process of inquiry, Stevenson became firmly wedded to his alternative explanatory theory, which was premised on the hereditarians' naturalistic

model of social structure. Therefore, consequent on his formulation of an apparently satisfactory alternative explanation of the causes of recent demographic change – diffusionism – Stevenson allowed himself, in the late 1920s, to emphasise the broad agreement between his theory and the form of social structure which it presupposed, by demonstrating how the demographic behaviour of the entire population, including the now embarrassing three industrial classes, could be subsumed within a model of five, neat, ordinal grades. (p. 538)

Szreter's account is exhaustive, explains the delay in introducing the SCS, fills in the gaps noted previously, and makes sense. From our point of view this means that Stevenson's adoption of the underlying characteristics of the hereditarian model of social structure is embedded in the basic form of the SCS which is still in use over half-a-century later(see Chapter 3). Whilst many social scientists use this scheme in their day-to-day labours, we hope that few espouse such a simplistic and theoretically nasty model.

2.4 JUSTIFYING THE CLASSIFICATION

We have said that Stevenson claimed that the observed fertility and mortality gradients constituted evidence for the soundness of the classification. As this kind of argument is also used currently (McDowell, 1981) to justify the continued use of the SCS, it is worth closer examination. Stevenson said:

> There is nothing new in the idea that mortality and fertility are higher in the lower than in the upper social grades. It is indeed so well established and confirmed by so much evidence of various kinds that its truth may be assumed. It seems then to follow that as low social status is a factor in high mortality, mortality should tend to rise as status falls in a case such as that under consideration where other factors influencing mortality, such as sex, race and climate, are substantially similar for all classes. If there were similarity of these other factors, variation of mortality would be due only to social status, and the death rates of the five classes would vary strictly in accordance with it. (pp. 212–13)

In effect, since other causes of mortality are, Stevenson suggests, randomly distributed among the social classes, the randomisation ought to ensure that class gradients reflect the effects of social status rather than the differential distribution of the other factors.

The validity of the social class scheme Stevenson derived, then, was tested by its association with mortality. Stevenson goes on to claim that the association between mortality and the groups derived provides evidence not only for the correctness of the social grading employed, but also for the association of excess mortality with lower social status:

> If the social classification used here were without validity there would be no reason for the correspondence with mortality. A chaotic grouping of the population would be as likely to exhibit high or low mortality in one section as in another. And, on the other hand, if there were no association with poverty (much more closely associated with low status than wealth with its opposite) and mortality, the graduation of mortality by occupationally distinguished sections of society would be inexplicable. (pp. 213–21)

At first sight the argument is extraordinary. Since social status is associated with mortality, a grouping of occupations which shows mortality gradients must, all other things being equal, reflect social status. Since the grouping of occupations which reflects social status shows mortality gradients, mortality is associated with social status. Indeed, Stevenson himself admits the argument is circular:

> All this evidence, I think, goes on to show that the social distinctions have been successfully drawn, and that they profoundly influence mortality as well as fertility. If this is granted, we can reverse the argument ... and proceed from the assumption of the correctness of the social distinctions made to examine the social distribution of mortality from various causes. (p. 215)

The argument, however, works rather better than such an account would imply. If one imagines that society is structured into a hierarchy of social positions, and that particular positions in that hierarchy are associated with particular sorts of occupations and levels of mortality, then mortality does provide a test of whether *particular* groupings of occupations successfully reflect broad groupings of social position. Of course, it would be possible, as was suggested by Stevenson (1928, p. 221), to simply rank occupations by mortality. Not only would that raise the problems of small numbers in certain occupational groups, but it would also entail the loss of any sense of social position in the analysis. Mortality, especially infant mortality where causes specific to the occupation are less immediate, is to be used as a general test for the grouping as a whole, not as a particular test to be applied to particular occupational units within the group. If, then, the mortality gradients displayed by the SCS groups reflect mortality gradients by social position in general, then, as Stevenson argued, the analysis of particular causes of mortality using the SCS groups would provide insight into the particular causes of mortality that are unequally distributed in society.

Given this line of argument, the accusation (Jones and Cameron, 1984) that Stevenson allowed his occupational grouping to be influenced by occupation-specific mortality rates is a damaging one. Had he ranked all occupations by mortality and chosen groups by 'cut-off' points within that ranking, the classes so generated would have been valuable for some sorts of epidemiological investigation. However, the test of the validity of the *social* grading of the occupations by mortality becomes invalid if the intuitive sense of social position was supplemented by knowledge of mortality in making the assignment of a particular occupation to a particular social class. On our reading, the case remains not proven.

2.5 CONCLUDING REMARKS

We have established that Stevenson's attempts to devise a personal classification of occupations was a failure. Stevenson saw the classification he developed as appropriate to the individual whilst recognising the possibility of misclassification; in fact he only really identified three main classes. He chose occupation rather than overcrowding or penury because it was relatively independent of the outcomes – fertility and mortality – in which he was interested. But this choice was intuitive, based on an implicit view of a social structure with an enduring and stable hierarchy and not on the basis of an empirical comparison of occupation (or its relationship to fertility and mortality) with other possible alternatives.

Further, Szreter (1984) shows how the eventual form of the SCS can best be understood in the context of the contemporary debate between the environmentalist conception of 'class' and hereditarian view of social structure. The SCS of 1913 was addressing the issue of national reproductive efficiency and was therefore organised in those terms. Whilst Stevenson did not accept the postulated deterioration in fecundity, he eventually did accept the hereditarians' naturalistic model of social structure, and that remains the only 'model' underlying the current SCS.

Finally, we show how Stevenson justified the *particular* grouping of occupations be reference to the overall grading of mortality that resulted. Although our reading of Stevenson would not support Jones and Cameron's accusations, their general point is worth noting. If the Office Population Censuses and Surveys (OPCS) scheme has been modified over the last few decades by reference to the mortality of particular occupations this would render the scheme hopelessly circular. In the next chapter we shall briefly discuss these modifications,

Notes

1. The decision that committee took to base the new occupational classification on the materials worked in and sub-dividing by process is, at first sight, very similar to the basis set out for the industrial classification in 1851. However, for the occupational classification, the occupational title still distinguishes between the manipulation of different kinds of material. It thus continued to contain references to the industry which, whilst serving the interests of epidemiologists concerned with some types of occupation-specific risks, meant that it was – is? – grounded in the interwar industrial structure.
2. Although, of course, household density data was available. The modern distinction between form of tenure only became of interest in late capitalism.
3. This peculiarly upper-class British disdain of money is part of the glorification of the amateur which has produced the British managerial disease, as well as an incomprehensible social class classification.
4. Although Stevenson uses the mortality of the clergy to support his feeling that such a ranking would be 'wrong', there is no suggestion here that mortality statistics were directly used to arrive at the assignment of occupations.
5. It is important to emphasise that this is different from the contemporary debate which is concerned with explaining and accounting for the differences in rates, especially mortality (see Townsend and Davidson, 1982; Whitehead, 1987); for although this also interested Stevenson, our interest is in the conceptual framework underlying the classification.
6. In the same period, Rowntree also used these notions to distinguish primary from secondary poverty. Primary poverty referred those whose income was just sufficient to buy the basic necessities; secondary poverty referred to those who, in principle, had sufficient income but spent it unwisely (Rowntree, 1937).
7. He reported a mortality rate of 28.2 per 1000 in the first five years of life among upper and middle classes, compared to 61.0 per 1000 among the 'lower' classes.
8. The different policy implications of environmentalist and hereditarian views of social inequality are dramatic. The environmentalists had argued consistently for the value of schemes of preventive sanitation and education directed at the poorest and most disadvantaged sections of the community. The hereditarian argument, on the other hand, suggested that resources should be directed at ensuring the interbreeding and healthy nurture of the fittest and most able sections of society. Galton (1901) was to discuss the actuarial calculations necessary to discover the sums of money it was legitimate to spend on favouring the highest classes (p. 664).

   In the hereditarian view, work aimed at improving the lot of the least advantaged sections of the population would be wasted. Pearson (1912) was to inveigh against the proposed (modest) legislation for maternity leave for women and pour scorn on the results of an experiment of nutritional supplementation for poor children. Improving the survival prospects of the children of the lower classes was to be, quite literally, viewed as encouraging the survival of the unfittest.

3 The Registrar-General's Social Class Scheme: The Last Half-Century

There have, of course, been modifications to the Registrar-General's SCS since 1921. The purpose of this chapter is to explore whether these modifications have affected the conceptual basis of the scheme.

3.1 MODIFICATIONS 1931–71

A major discontinuity resulted from the transfer of half-a-million male clerks from social class II to social class III; in 1911 they had been classified in social class I. The reduction in employment in many old established industries was the start of a long decline in the size of social class V; and the growing importance of the engineering and tertiary sector of the economy brought with it a growth of white collar and personal service occupations.

The subsequent growth of technology meant it became necessary for employees in many occupations to undergo extensive training and to obtain professional qualifications; the resultant improvement in social position meant they tended to climb the social scale. For example, there was a major revision in the 1960 Classification of Occupations, with aircraft pilots being reclassified from Social Class III to II, and postmen and telephone operators from Social Class III to IV. The overall effect of these changes between 1931 and 1971 are substantial, as can be seen from Table 3.1.

As Leete and Fox (1977) make clear, the major concern guiding changes in the classification scheme has been to preserve continuity from one census to another. This is an important consideration but it should not override the importance of providing a theoretical basis for the classifications. None of the reclassifications seem to have been guided by any theoretical consideration.

3.2 CLASSIFICATION BASED ON EMPLOYMENT STATISTICS

In parallel to these developments, government departments handling employment and vacancies have developed their own detailed classification

Table 3.1 Distribution* per 1000 of economically active and retired males by their own social class, 1931, 1951 and 1971 (England and Wales)

Social class	Age group	1931	1951	1971[†]
I	16–44	18	31	50
	45–64	32	33	41
II	16–44	100	119	143
	45–64	183	175	195
IIIN	16–44	511	563	109
	45–64	435	462	104
IIIM	16–44			355
	45–64			345
IV	16–44	184	150	138
	45–64	166	163	182
V	16–44	163	98	61
	45–64	171	153	81
All[‡]	16–44	1 000	1 000	1 000
Population (000s)		8 660.6	8 910.3	9 525.6
All[‡]	45–64	1 000	1 000	1 000
Population (000s)		4 068.4	4 902.4	5 722.4

[†] The lower age-group for 1971 was 15–44.
[‡] The *All* category included students and persons whose occupations were inadequately described as well as those who were unoccupied.
* The actual numbers (000s) are given as the *population*.

systems. The first was published in 1927 as the Dictionary of Occupational Terms. This remained essentially the same apart from minor modifications until a major revision undertaken in the 1960s, which led to the publication in 1972 of the Classification of Occupations and Directory of Occupational Titles (CODOT).

CODOT is a detailed and hierarchical system of classification with 18 Major and 73 Minor Groups, 378 Occupational Client Groups and 3800 'Occupations'. The main criteria for grouping jobs together are the nature of the tasks which the job entails, and detailed lists of tasks and of job titles are associated with each group. The associated Key list of Occupations for Statistical Purposes (KOS) contains 404 occupational categories which map directly into the CODOT Major Groups.

Evolution of the Social Class Scheme 27

Pressure was exerted upon OPCS to bring the system they used to classify census and other survey information into line with CODOT. As Thomas and Stanyer (1984) argue, considerations of interorganisational coordination predominate over issues of policy-relevance in the design of statistical systems. OPCS did introduce some new distinctions in their scheme and proposed a new Classification of Occupations for the 1981 Census (CO80). As many as 161 'Condensed Key list' categories were defined to be identifiable both via the 404 KOS categories and via CO80. The relationship is illustrated in Figure 3.1.

With this suite of changes, it would have been reasonable to expect a new theoretical justification for the classification, and indeed the *declared* criterion for classifications have changed. Thus, in 1970:

> The unit groups included in each of these categories have been selected so as to ensure that, so far as is possible, each category is homogeneous in relation to the basic criterion *of the general standing within the community* of the occupations concerned. The criterion is naturally correlated with, and its application conditioned by, other factors such as education and economic environment, but it has no direct relationship to the average level of remuneration of particular occupations. (OPCS, *Classification of Occupations*, 1970, p. x; our italics)

And in 1980:

> The occupation groups included in each of these categories have been selected in such a way so as to bring together, so far as is possible, *people with similar levels of occupational skill*. In general, each occupation group is assigned as a whole to one or another social class and no account is taken of differences between individuals in the same occupation group, e.g. differences of education or level of remuneration. (OPCS, *Classification of Occupations*, 1980, p. xi: our italics)

Boston (1980) writes of the purpose, origins and objectives of the classification of occupations to be used for analysing the 1981 Census. To those like us, searching for a theoretical justification, he starts encouragingly: 'Direct comparison between the 1911 and 1980 indexes is difficult because they are constructed on different principles' (p. 9). Unfortunately, this remains an enigmatic observation not elaborated upon in the remainder of his article. Indeed, apart from saying that the OPCS have based their 1981 classification on the 1972 version of CODOT, there is not even an explanation for the change in criterion from 'standing in the community' to 'skill'.

28 The Current Social Classification of Women

Figure 3.1 Present systems of occupational classification compared with the Standard Occupational Classification

Present classifications of occupations

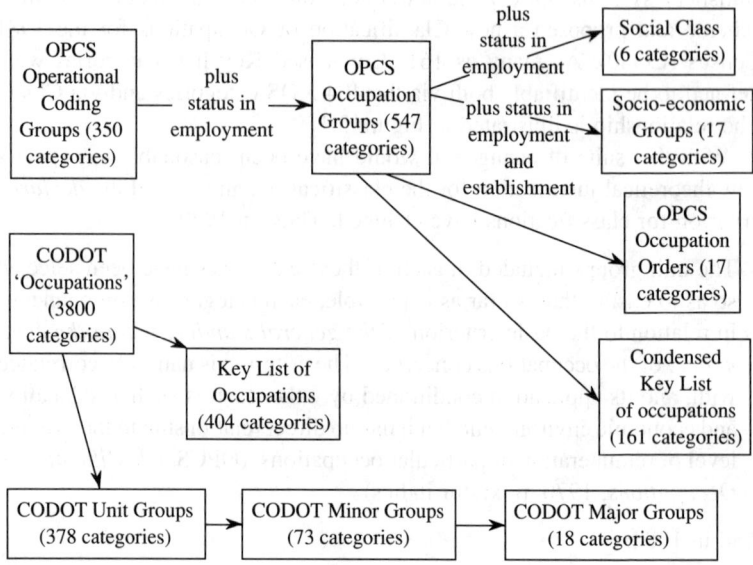

Standard Occupation Class

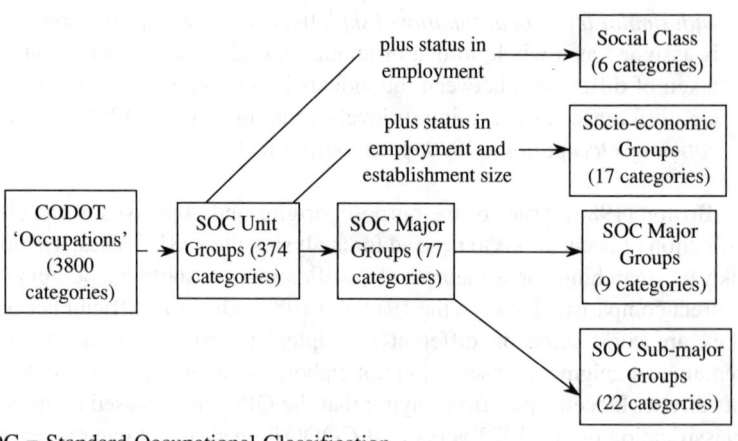

SOC = Standard Occupational Classification
- - - Indicates that a partial mapping (not 1:1) exists between the categories
——— Indicates that a unique mapping (1:1) exists between the categories

Evolution of the Social Class Scheme

The change ought to have had a profound effect on the structure of the classification, but the overall impression given is that the change in criterion is seen as cosmetic rather than substantial. For example, the classification rules were varied in precisely the same way for both foremen and managers in both 1970 and 1980, with no evidence that the skill levels of occupation vary in a corresponding fashion. The suggestion that there is an underlying continuity is reinforced by the fact that, in practice, the shift in 'meaning' does not seem to have had a substantial impact on the classifications.

When the 1980 Classification of Occupations was introduced, OPCS recoded a 1 per cent sample of 1971 Census records for employed men and women to the new classification. Table 3.2 summarises the shifts for men: in all, about 10 percent of men were allocated to different classes. Numerically, the three largest changes were the reclassification 'upwards' of 1.1 percent of men from IV to IIIM, and the reclassifications 'downwards' of 1.9 percent of men from IIIM to IV and of 1.0 percent of men from I to II.

The shift from an outward-looking reference from occupation to social status (standing in the community) to an inward-looking focus on skill levels within occupational groupings renders the current classification quite

Table 3.2 Census: recoded sample of employed men, 1970 and 1980 classifications (England and Wales)

1970 classification	1980 classification						All employed men
	I %	II %	IIIN %	IIIM %	IV %	V %	%
I	4.2	1.0	0.0	0.0	0.0	–	5.3
II	0.3	16.7	0.3	0.5	0.2	–	18.0
IIIN	0.1	0.5	11.0	0.2	0.1	0.0	11.9
IIIM	0.0	0.4	0.7	34.8	1.9	0.2	38.1
IV	0.0	0.1	0.4	1.1	14.8	0.6	17.1
V	–	–	0.0	0.4	0.3	6.6	7.3
All employed men	4.6	18.7	12.4	37.0	17.2	7.5	100.0

Note: Diagonal elements are underlined to indicate no change on recoding.

irrelevant, at least in principle, to debates about social inequalities in Britain (*pace* Whitehead, 1987; Wilkinson, 1986). Job skill may have been an indicator of social rank in the nineteenth century, but not now.

3.3 THE PROPOSED STANDARD OCCUPATIONAL CLASSIFICATION

In practice, the attempt at assimilation did not simplify the use of the classification scheme and only exacerbated the discontinuity between CO80 and its predecessor, CO70. Dissatisfaction with this situation, together with the move to update the International Standard Classification of Occupations (ISCO) by the International Labour Office, has led to the development of a common classification to be known as the Standard Occupational Classification (SOC), which would replace CO80 as well as CODOT.

It was agreed that the concept to be classified was that of 'a *job*' to be considered as a set of employment tasks. This is seen as different from classifying a *person* directly in terms of his or her skill or experience and is clearly very different, at least in intention, from classifying a person in terms of his or her social standing. Moreover, the SOC would be based entirely on information about the type of work done, as indicated by job title and job description. It would not be dependent upon 'ancillary' information about status in employment, because these are not available in all sources. From the point of view of users in the Employment Group of departments, the most useful criteria were related to the types and levels of skill, work experience, qualifications and training usually required to do the job.

The format of the classifications was to be hierarchical, allowing for four levels of aggregation. The idea was that classification should reflect important differences within the current spectrum of occupation and remove distinctions which had become obsolete through technical and industrial change. At the same time, a reasonable degree of compatibility was to be maintained with existing versions of the classifications and with the new version of ISCO and with CO80 in particular.

Finally, the new classifications were intended to be practical and reliable, both in client-oriented applications such as job-placement and vocational guidance. In some cases this meant that a consistent set of criteria for distinguishing differences and maintaining similarities between occupations could not always be maintained.

The aim was to adapt the structure of the 350 Operational Coding Groups used in CO80 to meet the SOC criteria. The proposed classification was tested for 'feasibility' against 0.5 percent of responses to the questions

Evolution of the Social Class Scheme 31

on occupation, status in employment, industry and qualifications in the 1981 Census; this led to some new discriminations and some proposals being abandoned. After 'field testing' of SOC in selected Job Centres, and consultation with users of OPCS data, the eventual result was a list of 374 SOC Unit Groups as compared with the 350 CO80 Operational Coding Groups and the 378 Unit Groups in CODOT.

However, despite the extensive technical back-up, the application of SOC criteria to placing an occupation in a particular category seems to have proceeded by consensual osmosis rather than conceptual praxis. We are no nearer knowing what social scale the SOC scheme is meant to reflect, and supposed tests of validity are often circular and should be assessed in that light (see Chapters 6 and 9).

It is clear that the adjustments and tinkerings between 1921 and 1971 have not been on the basis of a view of what a social class classification ought to indicate and therefore why an occupation should be reclassified or why a new occupation should be placed in a particular category. The new proposals, whilst moving away from the attempt to provide a social basis for the classification, do not provide an alternative theoretical basis and its only test of 'validity' is the extent to which the coding is reliable. In any case, this debate does not affect our analysis of data collected over the last 40 years.

3.4 A RÉSUMÉ: IS STEVENSON'S SOCIAL CLASS SCHEME RELEVANT TODAY?

It may seem strange in a study of the empirical problems of female social class to allocate so much space to a discussion of how one male classified many others of the same gender over 50 years ago. It seems to us, however, that attempts (including our own) to devise a system of classification appropriate to women which can be used with empirical data have many parallels with Stevenson. The problem is to make sense of data in the context of a specific set of theoretical debates. This was precisely Stevenson's problem: he wanted to manipulate Census and Vital Registration data to confront a hereditarian view of society.

We can therefore learn from Stevenson's endeavours. This review has made clear at least one very important methodological point about the art (rather than science) of devising a classification: classifications are usually designed in a particular context and for a specific purpose. Stevenson wanted to address an argument about the relative fertility and morality of the middle classes and the working classes. He chose groupings of occupations in accordance with the contemporary debate between herediterians and environmentalists; moreover, his crucial distinction between manual and non-manual was also a direct consequence of the terms of that debate. Anyone who uses the SCS should understand what they are using.

Furthermore, the review has shown that the SCS classification was not intended as a description of the social structure, even though its originator did eventually persuade himself that it was a useful tool in this sense. Clearly, therefore, it is even less likely to be appropriate today as a reflection of social and industrial structure, and the considerable effort put into the frequent modifications are of little help. Further, the modifications have not been designed on the basis of a coherent theoretical formulation. Indeed, recent attempts to rationalise the occupational building blocks of the scheme in terms of job content are reminiscent of the problems encountered in the late nineteenth and early twentieth century of resolving the competing demands of those interest in 'questions of vital statistics' and those concerned with 'questions of economics' (see Chapter 2).

We are therefore still dealing with a revision of Stevenson's classification. Whilst the SCS classification continues empirically to discriminate many outcomes, the SCS as proposed by Stevenson and propped up by many a writer thereafter is irrelevant to understanding the current everyday realities of poverty and wealth. In the next chapter, we examine how Stevenson – and, *a fortiori*, those using the SCS – dealt with women.

4 Women in the Social Class Scheme

4.1 INTRODUCTION

Until fairly recently, the standard practice in official uses of the SCS has been to assign women a social class according to the occupation of the 'head of the household' in which the women live. For practical purposes, this has meant that the social class of married women has been assigned on the basis of their husband's occupation. More recently, some attempt has been made to include tabulations based on the woman's own occupation coded according to the SCS.

Both bases have been the subject of criticism, the former because it subsumes the women's individual characteristics under those of her husband and the latter because it assumes both that a women's occupation is a useful measure of her social position and that the women's occupational market is similar to that for men. Oakley (1981) provides a neat summary:

> the woman's second-hand status in conventional analysis is both a reality and a lie. The reality is that women in advanced capitalist nations lack economic autonomy and are highly dependent on the uncertain male-determined fortunes of their functions as wives, mothers and housekeepers. The lie is that men's occupations are any index of women' occupations. (p. 289)

The intention of this chapter is to offer an account of how the method of assigning women's social class came about and to examine the main lines of criticism in more detail. Additional discussion of the problems raised by the method of classification is to be found in Chapters 6 and 7.

4.2 THE ORIGINS OF THE METHOD OF TREATMENT OF WOMEN IN THE SOCIAL CLASS SCHEME

By the time the SCS came to be formulated in the early years of this century, there was long standing interest at the GRO in the statistics of women's employment. The basic reason for this interest lay in the prevalent belief that the employment of women, especially those who were married with children, was a bad thing. Thus the Report of the 1851 Census notes:

34   The Current Social Classification of Women

'The duties of a wife, a mother and a mistress of a family can only be efficiently performed by unremitting attention; accordingly it is found that, in districts where women are much employed from home, the children and parents perish in great numbers' (p. lxxxviii). By the turn of the century, the relationship between women's employment and childhood mortality was accepted orthodoxy. In 1894, the then Registrar-General, Jones, summed up a review of the statistics in the following manner: 'The children of women engaged in industrial occupations suffer from the effects of maternal neglect. They are handicapped from the moment of birth in their struggle for existence, and have to contend, not only with the inevitable perils of infancy, but also against the perils due to neglect by their mothers' (p. 56).

In spite of this general interest and strongly held opinions on the subject, there were considerable practical difficulties in collecting women's occupational data. The reliability of data relating to the employment of women had been questioned in successive Census Reports from the first 'modern' Census of 1801 (Census Report I, p. ix) onwards. One reason for the difficulty was that women, apparently, tended to give their husband's occupations. Thus, for example, a special investigation by the GRO of those women who were reported as blacksmiths or whitesmiths in the Census of 1891 concluded of the anomalous returns that: 'The explanation is to be found in the fact that women not infrequently returned themselves by their husband's occupation' (p. 57).

Occupational mortality figures for women had never been reported (they started being reported for men in 1851). In 1895, Clara Collet reviewed the available statistics on the effects of women's occupations on their health and that of their children and concluded: 'With regard to health statistics I would merely point out that we have no official statistics connecting the industrial occupations of women and girls with its effects on health in a trustworthy manner' (Collet, 1902, p. 243).

An attempt was made for the Decennial Supplement of 1901 to analyse women's occupational mortality. However, it was found that, while over a third of women enumerated in the 1901 Census had occupations recorded, only 8 percent of those who died in the years 1900–2 were recorded as having occupations. This anomaly, which persists in current statistics (see Macfarlane, 1980; McDowell, 1981), made – and continues to make – any analysis practically worthless.

The lack both of a tradition of analysing women's occupational data and of the reliable relevant data which would make that possible may have influenced Stevenson in simply ignoring women in the initial formulation of the SCS. But, given his interest in fertility and infant mortality, his concentration on a male-based framework of analysis is curious, and Stevenson realises it:

> It may at first sight seem somewhat arbitrary to propose to leave females out of account in these calculations. But, in reality, they are not being left out of account, for nature has so arranged matters that potential (legitimate) fertility of husbands is determined almost entirely by the ages of their wives. Miners, marrying young wives, tend to have large families on this account (though not on this account alone) and the effects of the wife's age will be expressed in the natality record of her husband. It has always been found necessary to confine records of occupational mortality to the male sex ... but the record for the male will automatically take account of the mortality as well as the fertility of the female. (1928, p. 219)

Stevenson's argument is that legitimate fertility, as the product of a couple, is only affected by two attributes of the female partner; her age and her death. The notion that a woman's 'independent' social position may influence the fertility of the couple and hence (male) class fertility does not appear to have entered into Stevenson's conceptual scheme.

However, Stevenson was speculating about analysing female mortality using her husband's social class. The difficulty with the analysis of male occupational mortality is that it confounds the risks inherent in a particular job with other factors (conditions of life) associated with social position. Indeed Stevenson later commented:

> The effect of occupation upon male mortality is on the whole more indirect than direct – mortality is influenced more by the conditions of life than by the direct occupational risks entailed ... It would therefore be possible to tabulate the mortality of 6–7 million married women according to the occupation of their husbands. If this were done, we should, for the first time, obtain a measure of the indirect effect (which in the case of females at all events is almost entirely of chief importance) of occupation on mortality. This would not only be of importance for females, but would also provide a means of roughly differentiating between the two different types of occupational influence upon males. (Registrar-General, 1927, p xiv)

The practice of classifying women 'indirectly', then, came about for three main reasons:

1. because the development of the system for the routine collection of

official statistics did not include the development of a successful system of collecting relevant data about women;
2. in an attempt to resolve conundrums inherent in the classification of men;
3. because of the perception of women's 'place' in society by those responsible for the presentation of official statistics in the interwar years.

The last reason provides crucial support for the other two. Were it not for the belief that 'husbands and wives had similar life styles and were, by implication of the same Social Class' (Leete and Fox, 1977, p. 4), it would have been difficult to avoid the development of specific ways of classifying women. Moreover, the proposal to use the analysis of female mortality by husband's social class to distinguish the effects of the husband's conditions of life from those of his occupation upon his mortality was premised on the belief that 'conditions of life' were shared; a belief that had been implicit in the earlier analyses of fertility and infant mortality by (male) social class.

There is another important – statistical – consequence of the perceived place of women in society. As Collet (1902) implied, no one was particularly interested in the effects of working conditions upon women's health. This remains true; despite subsequent analysis and debate about how to *classify* women, it is still very difficult to document variations in their condition or situation. Quite simply, they are grossly under represented in official statistics (Nissel, 1980). Unsurprisingly, their treatment in a classificatory scheme is cavalier.

4.3 THE MIXED BASIS FOR ASSIGNING WOMEN TO A SOCIAL CLASS CLASSIFICATION UNDER THE SCS

The current practice for the majority of uses to which the SCS and its derivatives are put is, then, to classify women according to the occupation of the 'head of household'. In general, protocols for determining who is the head of household are such that, where it is at all possible, the head of household is a man (see, for example, Oakley and Oakley, 1979; Nissel, 1980). The SCS does not, therefore, provide a uniform basis for the classification of the population: men are classified according to their membership of a group defined by their occupation, and women are classified according to their membership of a group defined by their relationship with a man. Not only does the SCS fail to provide a uniform basis for the classification of the population as a whole, it also fails to provide a uniform basis for the classification of women. Whilst it is the case that the majority of adult women are married and living with their husbands, a substantial minority are not currently married and may live in a variety of different sorts of household.

The conceptual difficulties with this mixed basis of assignment are recognised (see Chapters 6 and 11), but it is often implied that the actual amount of confusion resulting from mixed assignment is not large; the majority of adult women are married and the position of the residue, who for the most part are classified by their own occupation, is relatively clear. To discover the extent to which the practice of assignment on the basis of the occupation of the head of household *actually* represents a 'mixed basis', we examined data from an OPCS survey ('The Height and Weight of British Adults'). The sample and data are described in more detail in Chapter 7, but here it is sufficient to note that this was a random sample of people between the ages of 18 and 64 and that it includes data on 5317 women. The distribution of the relationships of these women to the 'head' of the households in which they were living is shown in Table 4.1.

Whilst it is correct to say that the majority were wives of the head of household (just over two-thirds of them were), the remaining 31.3 percent are clearly more than numerically 'trivial'. The group who were not wives of the head of household were, for the most part, either head of household themselves (14.3 per cent) or daughters of the head of household (14.1 percent). The remaining 2.9 percent were scattered across households headed by sundry different relatives (1.4 percent) or non-relatives (1.4 percent).

Table 4.1 Women's relationship to head of household

Relationship to head of household	N	%
Head of household	762	14.3
Wife	3652	68.7
Daughter	751	14.1
Daughter-in-law	10	0.2
Mother	5	0.1
Mother-in-law	2	0.0
Sister	27	0.5
Granddaughter	4	0.1
Other relative	22	0.4
Not relative	75	1.4
Unknown	7	0.1

Source: Knight (1984).

As would be anticipated, the distribution of the relationship with the head of household varies with marital status (see Table 4.2). It is not uniquely the case that married women would be classified according to their husband's occupation, although the proportion classified on another basis would be small (2.3 percent). The change in OPCS protocols which normally allowed women to be classified as 'head' of a conjugal household (Nissel, 1980) has had only a very marginal effect. The majority of single women were living in their parental household (69.2 percent) and only 20 percent of single women would be classified according to their own occupation. The apparent anomaly of single 'wives' is explained by the difference between formal marital status and the inclusion of 'common-law' wives in the category 'wife'.[1] The figures show 88.9 percent of divorced, widowed or separated women were the head of the household in which they were living.

Although the broad pattern of the relationship to the head of household is what might be expected – married women living with their husbands, single women living with their parents and divorced, widowed or separated women heading their own households – this mixed basis is not followed uniformly. If we know a woman's marital status we still would not know on what basis she had been classified, and if we knew on what basis she had been classified we would not know her marital status. When the distribution

Table 4.2 Marital status of women and their relationship to the head of household

Relation of woman to head of household	Married (%)	Single (%)	Divorced/separated widowed (%)
Head of household	33 (0.9)	202 (20.0)	527 (88.9)
Wife	3 627 (97.7)	12 (1.2)	13 (2.2)
Daughter	27 (0.7)	699 (69.2)	25 (4.2)
Other	27 (0.7)	97 (9.6)	28 (4.7)
Total (100%)	3 714	1010	593

Source: Knight (1984).

of social classes, assigned on the basis of the occupation of the 'head' of household is examined, the following picture emerges (see Table 4.3).

There are differences in the social class distribution according to the basis of the classification, most markedly between those classified by their own occupations and those classified according to someone else's, but also according to who the 'someone else' is. It is possible to tell stories that 'account' for these variations in the class distribution. The differences in structure between male and female labour markets would account for the relatively high proportion of IIIN amongst those classified by their own occupations. The relatively high proportion of 'unclassified' in this group might be explained by the fact, noted above, that the majority of this group are previously married and may have child-care responsibilities which make working difficult. The differences between parental and husband's class distributions may be regarded as generational differences, reflecting intergenerational changes in the employment market, differences in the length of time parents and husbands have been in employment and the rather higher proportion of parents who have retired or are unable to work because of sickness or disability. The relatively high proportion of social classes I and II in the 'other' category may reflect the fact that the occupa-

Table 4.3 Women's social class: assigned by different associative ruler

Assigned social class	Classified by the occupation of:				Total sample Percentage % (N)
	Self % (N)	Husband % (N)	Parent % (N)	Other % (N)	
I and II	13.9 (106)	24.7 (903)	20.2 (152)	28.9 (44)	22.7 (1205)
IIIN	21.5 (164)	10.3 (377)	10.9 (82)	13.2 (20)	12.1 (643)
IIIM	8.3 (63)	41.6 (1 519)	37.7 (283)	30.3 (46)	35.9 (1911)
IV and V	25.2 (192)	16.9 (618)	18.2 (137)	18.4 (28)	18.3 (975)
Unclassified	31.1 (237)	6.4 (235)	12.9 (97)	9.2 (14)	11.0 (583)
Total sample percentage	14.3 (762)	68.7 (3 652)	14.1 (751)	2.9 (152)	100 (5317)

Note: Sample size in parenthesis.
Source: Knight (1984).

tions classed as I and II may require greater geographical mobility, which means that living arrangements tend to be less 'standard' and may themselves be 'class' phenomena.

However, although we can tell specious stories, appealing to gender and generational differences in labour markets and the fact that living arrangements may reflect social class, we do not actually know how these differences come about. The different bases that are used for the assignment come up with different distributions which are commonly lumped together for the purposes of analysis. We cannot finally say whether these differences are artefacts of the basis of assignment or reflect 'real' social phenomena. If as an act of blind faith, we assert that they reflect 'real' social phenomena, we cannot say which social phenomena are implicated.

In summary, the mixed basis of assignment is empirically significant, both in terms of the numbers involved and because of the variations in the distribution of social classes according to the different bases of assignment. Commonly, we do not know the mixture of bases of assignment used in government or research reports, and information about formal marital status only partially solves the problem. The complex relationships between the bases of assignment and a gender- and age-differentiated labour market only add to the confusion. The fact that there is not a unique satisfactory way of classifying women by occupation (whether their own or that of a convenient, proximate male) is no argument for the cavalier combination of bases of assignment.

4.4 WHAT IF WOMEN COUNTED?

Even if assignment by the occupation of the head of household was felt to provide a coherent basis for the classification of women, the question arises as to whether it is legitimate to use the head of household's occupation as the unique indicator of the household's social position and whether it is reasonable to use women's membership of a household to adduce their social position.

The current debate on these points focuses on two aspects: first on the degree of class homogamy (that is, whether women marry into the 'same' class so that we can take their individual class position from their husbands). This requires detailed examination of empirical data and is taken up in Chapter 5. Second, it also focuses or whether women's employment 'matters' and, if so, how it should be taken into account when classifying either individuals or households.

4.4.1 Does Women's Employment Matter?

There is no doubt that there currently exists a substantial proportion of 'dual-earner' households in the population and that, with the exception of a lull in the first Thatcher dynasty, the proportion has been steadily increasing. Thus, in the 1961 Census, 32 percent of wives of husbands who were economically active were themselves economically active. This proportion increased to 47 percent in 1971 and to 60 percent in 1981; according to the General Household Survey (1990), the estimated proportion was 70 percent in 1988. If the SCS is thought of as an indicator of relative 'conditions of life' (rather than as a tool for 'class analysis' in Goldthorpe's (1984) sense), the consequences of an increasing proportion of dual-earner families are that the amount of intraclass variation will increase. Households classified in a particular way according to the husband's social class will show a greater range of variation in income than would be implied in the (already considerable) range of incomes associated with the male occupations comprising the social class. The relative prosperity of dual-earner families will, inevitably, be reflected in their conditions of life and the resources that such families have to call upon in times of crisis.

This will be the case whether or not the occupations of both partners would be coded as the same social class. Thus a household with both a postwoman and a postman contributing to the income will be 'better off' than a household with only a postman's income. Of course, the equation is by no means simply additive: dual-earner households may incur additional expenditure (for example, child care) as well as receiving additional income. Nevertheless, in general, the net effect will tend to be positive.

The effects of women's employment are not confined to detracting from the value of the husband's occupation as a unique indicator for the household. There are also consequences for the woman's life (Poulten and Heath, 1982). The distribution of household income and control over expenditure is by no means simple to assess, but it does seem to be the case that, whatever the husband's social class, women have fewer resources for 'personal' expenditure than their husbands (Pahl, 1980; Pahl, 1983; Whitehead, 1981). The marginal effects of married women's employment seem more likely to increase the resources they have available in their 'own right' than, for example, an equivalent increase in their husband's earnings (see Syson and Young, 1974). Furthermore, the patterns of sociability and the division and nature of household labour differ between working and non-working wives. The way in which a woman's membership of a household indicates something about the woman, differs according to whether or not she is in employment.

Classifying women according to their husband's social class in the belief that, as a unique indicator, it provides valuable or interpretable aggregate information about differential life chances among women, simply does not work in circumstances where a substantial proportion of women are in employment and a substantial proportion are not. The husband's social class does not adequately indicate the relative resources available to the household. The lives of married women, in terms of their independent command over resources and, simply, how they spend their time, differ according to whether or not they 'go out to work'. This is not to deny that the life chances of married women are powerfully affected by their marriage in our society and differ substantially according to the social classes of the men they marry (see Chapter 8). The argument is, rather, that because of the differences between dual- and single-earner households and between married women who work and those who do not, a view of the social distribution of life chances based solely on a classification of the employment of the husband is, at best, partial and not amenable to unambiguous interpretation.

It may, instead, be argued that the aspects of inequality which are addressed by social class are not primarily related to financial resources. Stevenson's avowed intention, after all, was to find an indicator of what he called 'culture', which he specifically distinguished from prosperity. In contemporary terms, we are concerned with status and not solely with wealth.

4.4.2 How Should it be Taken into Account?

Essentially, the defence of the use of husband's occupation to classify wives relies on one of three presumptions. The Registrar-General's SCS may be an adequate description of the class structure of society *a priori*, in which case no empirical argument is relevant. Whilst that might be a theoretically comfortable position for some, it is difficult to maintain given the history of the SCS and the arguments reviewed above. Then again, because of the vagaries of current recording practices (for example, of female occupations), the husband's occupation may simply be the most reliable indicator of the woman's class position. Indeed, none of the criticisms of this basis of classification is intended to deny the importance of husbands, or of husbands' social class, for the lives of married women in our present society. For example, McDowell's (1981) paper based on the Longitudinal Survey data confirms, yet again, that husbands' social class is a better indicator of inequalities in mortality than social class based on women's own occupations. In other words, the SCS *works* for women. But there is a third position which needs to be considered before we turn in Part II to examine the empirical basis for this argument, for one could argue that patterns of female employment (and patterns of any other female activity for that matter) grow out of the class position of the family or household, rather than vice versa. Moreover, the direct use of patterns of employment for married females as an indicator of the class position of the household would be complicated by the predominant tendency for women to move in and out of the labour market at different stages of family building. The greater 'commitment to, and continuity in, [the] labour market' (Goldthorpe, 1983, p. 470) of the husband would make his occupation a more reliable indicator of the *household's*) class position.

In this defence, the potential value of the husband's social class as an indicator of his wife social class depends, crucially, upon the belief that conjugal households can be regarded as a 'cultural' (in Stevenson's sense) unit. Once that belief is accepted, because the husband is a member (in some versions the predominant member) of that unit, something which is a fair indicator of his 'culture' will be a fair indicator of the 'culture' of the unit as a whole. Since the wife is also a member of that unit it will be a fair indicator of her 'culture'.

Although it seems reasonable to reject the belief that the family is a cultural unit immediately on the grounds that it is absurdly simplistic, the debate about whether or not the belief can be maintained has tended to centre on the extent to which marriages are, in fact, class (social class) homogamous. Do women, in fact, marry socially (culturally)? That is the subject of the next chapter.

Note

1. The concern to differentiate married and common-law wives is becoming redundant. In Sweden, for example, there are few, if any, differences between women who are married or are cohabiting (see, for example, Hoem and Rennermalm, 1985); indeed, the classification of marital status is not typically collected for official statistics in Sweden.

5 Do Women Marry Socially?

The main 'theoretical' justification[1] for using husband's social class as an index for their unfortunate spouses therefore rests on the empirical claim that marriages are on the whole homogamous by social class. The difficulty with testing that claim – suspending, for the purposes of this chapter, our doubts about what the SCS is actually an index of – is that some independent indicator of a woman's social class is obviously essential to that argument: that is, even assuming that we *know* that the husband's social class reflects his social position, we have to find a similar index for the woman in order to test the claim that marriages are class homogamous. Of course, if we had such an index, the question of class homogamy would not arise in this context!

5.1 MARITAL SOCIAL CLASS

The main contenders for an index for (potential) wives in order to examine social class patterns of marriage have been either the woman's father's occupation or her own occupation. When the latter is used, the woman's premarital occupation is generally preferred to her current occupation because a woman's employment history may be affected by the fact of her marriage or by the pattern of family building. Whichever is used, it should be emphasised that each is subject to the criticism of the previous two chapters.

There are other (technical) difficulties inherent in using male and female pre-marital occupations to assess the extent of social class homogamy. As regards male occupations, the data of marriage represents one point (early) in a career 'trajectory'. Figures from the Scottish Mobility Study (Payne and Payne 1981) show that the period between the ages of 18 and 27, which would cover the majority of marriages, is one of marked upward mobility between the social classes. Of itself, this would not detract from patterns of social class homogamy or heterogamy at the time of marriage. However, the upward mobility that is characteristic of those ages is more pronounced among men from non-manual backgrounds (that is with fathers in social classes I, II or IIIN) than among men from manual backgrounds. This would suggest that there are factors present at the time of marriage (indicated

Do Women Marry Socially?

by social class background which may affect both the pattern of marriage and the eventual social class position of the husband. This 'mobility history' also poses a problem for the use of the woman's pre-marital occupation, although the assessment of her post-marital career is complicated by the fact of her marriage.

Apart from this difficulty, the use of women's pre-marital occupations is rendered more difficult by the fact that a relatively high proportion of brides do not have an occupation. Thus in a recent study (Haskey, 1987), just over 13 percent of spinster brides did not have an occupation at the time of marriage. Either these brides are excluded from the analysis or the bride's father's occupation is substituted. Haskey (1987) presents figures using both bases, but most fully for that where the bride's father's occupation is used for 'missing data'.

On that basis, excluding 'armed forces' and 'other' categories, 29.1 percent of marriages were class homogamous: if social classes I and II and, separately, IV and V are combined, 34.9 percent of marriages were class homogamous and, if a simple manual/non-manual dichotomy is used, 57.6 percent of marriages were homogamous. None of these figures would provide a basis for assigning wives to their husbands' social classes on the grounds of class homagamy.

Further inspection of the figures reveals a particular difficulty with using the women's own occupation as a basis for assigning her independent social class. While 44.6 percent of spinster brides were assigned to social class IIIn, only 14.0 percent of bachelor bridegrooms were; while 33.9 percent of bachelor bridegrooms were assigned to social class IIIm only 8.6 percent of spinster brides were; and over a third of the brides assigned to social class IIIm were assigned to that class on the basis of their fathers' occupations. The different structures of the male and female employment markets mean that, if the manual/non-manual division is to be maintained, using the woman's own occupation to assign her independent social class will tend to result in a picture of heterogamy,

An alternative basis, used by Berent (1954), Coleman (1977) and reported by Haskey (1987) is to use the bride's father's occupation to assign her to a social class. This basis at least has the advantage of being based entirely on male occupations, although it assigns the woman on a 'second-hand' basis and will reflect intergenerational differences in employment. From Haskey's (1987) figures it is not possible to adduce the proportions of marriages that were homogamous on this basis. However, he does report the ratio of observed to expected in 'homogamous' cells of the cross-classification with the χ^2 statistic for the whole table. On the basis of the figures, it is apparent that the degree of class homogamy revealed by the use of the bride's father's social class is lower than for either of the methods using the bride's own occupation.

It could, however, be argued that whilst there is no one-to-one relationship between either the wife's father's occupation or her own pre-marital occupation and the husband's occupation, that the departures from homogamy are patterned so as to reflect the woman's achieved social status.

In other words, despite social class heterogamy, the man and woman meet as a 'cultural unit' – at least in occupational terms – in the husband's social class. Whilst this is obviously a more complex position than the original 'cultural unit' argument requiring, *inter alia*, the 'hidden hand' of social mobility, it has the merit of relying on the same basic classification of occupations. However, in practice, this approach is affected by shifts in occupational structure, changes in the classification and intergenerational mobility.

In spite of all these difficulties, there is clearly some intuitive appeal to the 'meeting of bodies' argument, when the 'marriage market' is, at least in part, open. The point is: is it 'empirically true'?

5.2 THE WEE LADDIE NEXT DOOR?

There have been a variety of studies where sufficiently detailed data has been collected to test this kind of claim, but it is very difficult to compare them as the studies were conducted at different times (and in different places) and we know that, at least superficially, the status of women and the importance of their occupation has changed considerably over the last 30 years. Yet it is important for this defence of occupation-based measures of social class that they describe past, present and probable future patterns of marriage. The only study where consistent data has been collected across several time periods is the AMNDB.

The basic results about 'homogamy' are the three-way tabulations of husband's social class with the wife's father's occupation and with the wife's own pre-marital occupation. These are presented at the end of the chapter in Tables 5.1(a) and 5.1(c) (cf. Glass 1954). The question is whether the tendency to class homogamy means that the husband's occupational class summarises any of the other information that we have about the woman's class (subject to all the foregoing doubts and caveats). By inspection, this does not seem to be the case: a more rigorous test is provided by a simple log-linear analysis . We can ask whether omitting second- or higher-order interactions between husband's occupational class and either father's social class or the wife's own pre-marital occupation gives a good account of the pattern of variation in the data. As Table 5.1 shows, the assumption of class homogamy does not provide a good account of the variation in the multi-way table.

The hypothesis that the pattern of association does not vary over time can be tested by omitting the third- and higher-order interactions which include time and husband's social class. Again, this model does not fit the data (Chisquared = 456.59, degrees of freedom = 224 ($p < 0.001$)); the pattern of association in the tables varies over time. Although it may be the case that 'class homogamy is the predominant pattern of marriage', there is considerable variation round the pattern.

One could go on to argue that the empirical 'inconsistencies' in the marriage patterns could be accounted for by other factors reflecting the separate but targeted development of the potential spouses. Thus there have been several analyses of social mobility which have highlighted the effect of education upon carrier chances (such as Heath, 1981); and there have been arguments that female social mobility is related to a healthy development as measured by achieved adult height (Illsley, 1955). But, whilst it might be pleasant to speculate how we could use these relationships to operate a marriage bureau with a fair chance of providing the answer to a bachelor's or maiden's prayer, it misses the point. Accounting for, or explaining (or even interpreting) the pattern of marriages is one thing; constructing an indicator or measure which adequately captures a phenomenon is another.

For that purpose, the argument that the household is sufficiently homogenous in social class terms that the husband's occupation can be used as a reliable indicator for both spouses is weak. Social class homogamy – even when extended to include the woman's pre-marital occupation – does not provide a basis for assigning a woman to the social class of her husband. Patterns of marriage do not reveal conjugal families as 'cultural units' when social class is used as an indicator of 'culture'.

Table 5.1 Goodness-of-fit statistics for different models testing homogamy hypotheses

Second- and higher-order interactions omitted: husband's social class with:	Likelihood χ^2	Degrees of freedom (p)
Woman's father's occupation	3 672.23	256 ($p < 0.001$)
Woman's own occupation	2 700.92	240 ($p < 0.001$)

The only remaining justification for using husband's social class to represent the social status of their unfortunate spouses is that *in practice* – perhaps partially because of homogamy – as an index,[2] it works (compare Fox, 1984). *Compared to other possible indices*, HORG is the most useful index. There are several ways of examining the usefulness of a classificatory index, both methodological and pragmatic. Fundamentally, however, the utilitarian assessment of the value of an index is an empirical question in any given context. Part II examines this issue in the context of our efforts to describe and discriminate between mothers in respect of their own health and morbidity: a context rather similar to that of Stevenson.

Notes

1. In inverted commas because it is, in fact, almost entirely empirical.
2. The crude distinction being made here is between a theoretically-based indicator of a phenomenon and an empiricially useful index (see also Chapter 9).

Table 5.1(a) Three-way cross tabulation of husband, wife and wife's father's occupation, 1956–60

Wife's Father's Occupation = I or II

		Husband's occupation					
		I + II	IIIN	IIIM	IV + V	Unassigned	Total
	I + II	109	25	28	4	0	166
	IIIN	59	55	90	11	3	218
Wife's	IIIM	27	30	83	21	3	164
occupation	IV + V	7	4	18	19	7	55
	Unassigned	0	1	3	2	0	6
	Total	202	115	222	57	13	609

Do Women Marry Socially?

Wife's Father's Occupation = IIIN

		Husband's occupation					
		I + II	IIIN	IIIM	IV + V	Unassigned	Total
	I + II	27	9	9	1	0	46
	IIIN	49	53	96	18	3	219
Wife's	IIIM	12	23	72	30	2	139
occupation	IV + V	0	6	25	19	0	50
	Unassigned	1	1	1	0	3	6
	Total	89	92	203	68	8	460

Wife's Father's Occupation = IIIM

		Husband's occupation					
		I + II	IIIN	IIIM	IV + V	Unassigned	Total
	I + II	45	21	28	2	0	96
	IIIN	89	130	318	52	7	596
Wife's	IIIM	50	127	441	166	12	796
occupation	IV + V	5	15	198	116	11	345
	Unassigned	4	2	8	2	1	17
	Total	193	295	993	338	31	1850

Wife's Father's Occupation = IV + V

		Husband's occupation					
		I + II	IIIN	IIIM	IV + V	Unassigned	Total
	I + II	23	16	23	7	0	69
	IIIN	35	69	172	57	5	338
Wife's	IIIM	27	97	390	218	20	752
occupation	IV + V	7	38	256	219	33	553
	Unassigned	0	0	6	4	3	13
	Total	92	220	847	505	61	1 725

Wife's Father's Occupation = Unassigned

		Husband's occupation					
		I + II	IIIN	IIIM	IV + V	Unassigned	Total
	I + II	12	1	4	2	1	20
	IIIN	7	8	8	7	1	31
Wife's	IIIM	4	10	32	15	7	68
occupation	IV + V	1	0	22	18	13	54
	Unassigned	2	1	3	3	2	11
	Total	26	20	69	45	24	184

The Current Social Classification of Women

Table 5.1(b) Three-way cross-tabulation of husband, wife and wife's father's occupation, 1966–70

Wife's Father's Occupation = I + II

		Husband's occupation					
		I + II	IIIN	IIIM	IV + V	Unassigned	Total
Wife's occupation	I + II	156	31	34	14	5	240
	IIIN	71	63	114	45	14	307
	IIIM	45	23	83	35	14	200
	IV + V	4	4	19	20	7	54
	Unassigned	29	3	5	0	4	41
	Total	305	124	255	114	44	842

Wife's Father's Occupation = IIIN

		Husband's occupation					
		I + II	IIIN	IIIM	IV + V	Unassigned	Total
Wife's occupation	I + II	43	8	17	3	1	72
	IIIN	25	35	49	27	13	149
	IIIM	11	17	40	21	7	96
	IV + V	1	2	17	9	4	33
	Unassigned	11	0	1	1	1	14
	Total	91	62	124	61	26	364

Wife's Father's Occupation = IIIM

		Husband's occupation					
		I + II	IIIN	IIIM	IV + V	Unassigned	Total
Wife's occupation	I + II	97	22	37	14	4	174
	IIIN	117	119	299	136	54	725
	IIIM	67	58	287	156	76	644
	IV + V	8	12	117	102	67	306
	Unassigned	15	2	5	7	5	34
	Total	304	213	745	415	206	1 883

Do Women Marry Socially? 51

Wife's Father's Occupation = IV + V

		Husband's occupation					
		I + II	IIIN	IIIM	IV + V	Unassigned	Total
	I + II	50	15	36	7	6	114
	IIIN	90	75	266	104	49	584
Wife's	IIIM	42	50	344	250	66	752
occupation	IV + V	6	17	223	255	98	599
	Unassigned	3	2	7	2	2	16
	Total	191	159	876	618	221	2 065

Wife's Father's Occupation = Unassigned

		Husband's occupation					
		I + II	IIIN	IIIM	IV + V	Unassigned	Total
	I + II	18	4	3	2	6	33
	IIIN	11	17	24	11	13	76
Wife's	IIIM	5	3	24	10	20	62
occupation	IV + V	0	0	23	21	27	71
	Unassigned	9	2	0	0	4	15
	Total	43	26	74	44	70	257

Table 5.1(c) Three-way cross-tabulation of husband, wife and wife's father's occupation, 1976–80

Wife's Father's Occupation = I + II

		Husband's occupation					
		I + II	IIIN	IIIM	IV + V	Unassigned	Total
	I + II	205	25	48	24	15	317
	IIIN	85	34	70	67	16	272
Wife's	IIIM	18	12	45	27	11	113
occupation	IV + V	11	6	18	26	10	71
	Unassigned	67	16	25	12	16	136
	Total	386	93	206	156	68	909

The Current Social Classification of Women

Wife's Father's Occupation = IIIN

		Husband's occupation					
		I + II	IIIN	IIIM	IV + V	Unassigned	Total
	I + II	62	10	16	6	6	100
	IIIN	24	15	46	23	7	115
Wife's	IIIM	12	3	18	10	2	45
occupation	IV + V	4	1	9	11	6	31
	Unassigned	18	5	3	7	1	44
	Total	120	34	92	57	32	335

Wife's Father's Occupation = IIIM

		Husband's occupation					
		I + II	IIIN	IIIM	IV + V	Unassigned	Total
	I + II	87	26	53	29	5	200
	IIIN	109	61	226	135	49	580
Wife's	IIIM	35	19	166	103	46	369
occupation	IV + V	17	6	118	114	57	312
	Unassigned	22	7	31	24	18	102
	Total	270	119	594	405	175	1 563

Wife's Father's Occupation = IV + V

		Husband's occupation					
		I + II	IIIN	IIIM	IV + V	Unassigned	Total
	I + II	76	25	52	30	9	192
	IIIN	66	53	176	134	25	454
Wife's	IIIM	26	23	138	106	42	335
occupation	IV + V	24	14	127	206	89	460
	Unassigned	15	11	15	25	21	87
	Total	207	126	508	501	186	1 528

Wife's Father's Occupation = Unassigned

		Husband's occupation					
		I + II	IIIN	IIIM	IV + V	Unassigned	Total
	I + II	18	5	9	13	8	53
	IIIN	19	16	28	24	4	91
Wife's	IIIM	4	5	36	28	16	89
occupation	IV + V	6	8	32	58	25	129
	Unassigned	6	2	5	10	8	31
	Total	53	36	110	133	61	393

Part II
Constructing a Social Classification for Women

PROLOGUE

The chapters in Part I have shown how the occupationally-based SCS, at the time of its development, had no theoretical justification and very little empirical foundation. The extension of the SCS to the classification of women compounds the problems of the Scheme as a whole and, in particular, leads to questions about the universal appropriateness of an occupation-based index, especially for women.

Nevertheless, it is widely used as an index in empirical studies. Indeed, this apparent ability to discriminate a whole range of socially valued outcomes is its only remaining justification (see McDowell, 1981, and a contrary view from Fox, 1984). A defender of the SCS could argue, on entirely pragmatic grounds, that it does point to some distinguishing features – although we do not know precisely what, or exactly how to find out – and that there is nothing to replace it.

We have demonstrated that any theoretical reference in Stevenson's analysis was only implicit and that the application for women was entirely *ad hoc*: therefore the issue is not whether another index has a sounder theoretical basis than the Registrar-General's SCS, because it has not got one. Despite erudite justifications of the dominance of class by, for example, Goldthorpe (1984), the practice of applying the SCS to women in empirical studies depends entirely on its utility. The purpose of Part II is to dissect and examine this final solution. Whilst the argument is developed on the basis of our specific empirical problem – how best to classify women in order to analyse the distribution of pregnancy-related outcomes in a large data base over 30 years – we go on to show how it applies across the board.

Thus the first chapter in this part sets out the desirable criteria which should be fulfilled by an empirically useful classificatory tool in general. We then discuss the various options that were available to us and argue that, relative to the desirable criteria, HORG/SCS falls down badly, and that amongst our data, women's own height best satisfies these criteria. Admittedly, HORG/SCS has some face validity as an indicator of social position while height has none; however, it does provide a convenient tool for methodological exposition.

This chapter also starts the empirical argument by evaluating the relative discriminatory power of SCS and of woman's height *vis-à-vis* fertility and infant mortality: the two characteristics with which Stevenson himself was most concerned. We show that, in contemporary data, woman's height provides equally good discriminating power.

Of course, this is not a novel – or even a powerful – finding. We expected that height would be linked to sociobiological outcome variables of this kind. The arguments in favour of the SCS are much stronger; it usually discriminates a whole range of *other* socially valued outcomes.

The second chapter in this part argues that, whilst this is empirically correct, a useful index should be defined in relation to a *predefined* set of valued outcomes or, if you like, female life chances. It is rather too easy to argue *post hoc* that the SCS is useful when it discriminates and inappropriate when it does not. We therefore search for measures of a woman's happiness, health and status, which will probably include some concern with the welfare of her family. The choice of indicators is, of course, constrained by the data available to us.

The third chapter in the sequence lays out the corresponding empirical argument by simply comparing the discriminatory power of women's own height with that of the HORG classification based on the occupation of her husband's and with that of a 'pure' husband's occupation together, of course, with many unassigned. Given that there is no powerful theoretical reason to prefer HORG/SCS to women's own height (or any other characteristics), the issue is only *how* useful is HORG/SCS – relative to other contenders – in displaying variation and, with luck, pointing towards an explanation of variation. We show that, whilst HORG and the pure husband's occupation classification are both sometimes spectacularly good discriminators, they are erratic, and this is especially a problem with the unassigned 'class'. Women's own height, whilst less statistically powerful, is nearly always more consistent.

6 Classification Using HORG and the Alternative

This set of three chapters assesses the value of the claim that HORG works empirically as an index to discriminate a whole range of socially valued outcomes. For an indicator of social classness can 'work' without helping us to understand what is happening. This may arise because – as with the SCS – the indicator is not derived coherently and systematically or because it fails to fulfil simple technical criteria. The purpose of this, the first chapter in the sequence, is to discuss the extent to which SCS meets the technical criteria for index construction and then to consider the possible options which were available to us for analysis.

6.1 TECHNICAL CRITERIA FOR AN INDEX

Probably the most common mistakes is *reification* of an index: the substitution of the variable directly measured by the index for the underlying concept or phenomenon which the index is meant to be indicating. In particular, in many reports (for example, Dowding, 1981; Heath, 1981) SCS is used not only as an *index* to portray differences and/or inequalities but that portrayal is *also* assumed to constitute an explanation of those differences and/or inequalities. There are, of course, many reports that do not make that assumption: the Black Report on Inequalities in Health (Townsend and Davidson, 1982) is exemplary in that respect, proffering four possible explanations for an observed Registrar-General's social class distribution. But they have difficulty in maintaining the distinction between those explanations and 'social classness'; one political consequence was that a hostile government found it easy to ignore their findings (these difficulties were cited by Patrick Jenkin, Secretary of State for Social Services, 1980, as one of the reasons for not endorsing their recommendations), which is a high cost for methodological sophistication.

This points to the fundamental problem with using SCS as an index: it leaves investigators profoundly unclear as to what it is they know and bereft of the important sense of what it is that they do not know. Yet the way a classification operates ought to be unambiguous or, as a minimum requirement, relatively easy to describe. If one is trying to establish the extent to which social classness 'accounts' for the observed distribution or patterns of life chances, then indicators used to portary those distributions (such as SCS or HORG) should ideally clarify the causal mechanisms and, at the very least, not render them more opaque.

These problems illustrate a very important feature of a 'good' classifier: if the indicator is proposed as, of itself, explanatory, the nature of the explanation should be unambiguous. There are no easy ways to avoid these problems completely but there are some technical criteria which should be fulfilled by any indicator and these are discussed in the remainder of this section.

6.1.1 A Sound Index

The indicator proposed should not be *circular:* that is, the evidence produced to justify a causal link should not itself rely on the *explicandum*. For example, this group of people are poor because they are in social class V; they are in social class V because they are poor. Again, the tabulation of educational attainment by social class of head of household shows a typical gradient, but the juxtaposition of observations that 'you have a social class V occupation because you are poorly educated' and 'Your lack of education is typical of those in social class V' does not constitute the basis of an explanation. This may seem trivial. However, we showed how Stevenson fell into this trap when attempting to validate his proposed scheme. The evidence he gives for the validity of SCS as a reflection of social distinctions is that it discriminates mortality. He then claims that, because SCS is a valid mirror of society, we can go on to examine the social process bringing about differential mortality (compare with section 2.3 above).

The basis of the classification of the indicator should be 'pure'. For example, the use of tenure *as an index of social classness* could not be validated by showing that tenure discriminates access to amenities. A household's tenure directly affects its access to amenities, so we cannot tell if there is any effect upon access to amenities due to social classness rather than to tenure. Stevenson was greatly concerned with this problem and accordingly rejected several other possible alternatives to occupation as the basis for SCS. He recognised that it was *also* a problem when using his own occupation-based classification to discriminate mortality, because some jobs were in themselves dangerous, so that the observed differential mortality on the basis of his occupationally-based scheme was a combination of a pure 'social class' effect and an effect due to the risks associated with the occupation: and, as noted in Chapter 4 above, this led to his attempt to isolate the 'pure' social class effect by looking at the mortality of wives by the occupational group of their husbands. Whilst the problem of circularity is usually relatively easy to avoid and detect, the problem of 'impurity', like that of 'reification', is much more difficult. It is difficult to steer a course between the Scylla of ambiguous profusion and the Charybdis of meaningless clarity. It is important to ensure that indices have a clear relation to the phenomenon being indicated: in another context, Townsend has made the same point:

> It is, we believe, mistaken to treat being a member of an ethnic minority as part of the definition of deprivation. Even if many among this minority are deprived, some are not and the point is to find out how many *are* deprived rather than operate as if all were in that condition. It is the form their deprivation takes and not their status which has to be measured. (Townsend, Phillimore and Beattie, 1986, p. 21)

6.1.2 A Meaningful Index

Apart from conceptual considerations, there are some technical prerequisites about the nature of a classification for a classification. Technically speaking, there should be a *uniform* basis for the classification; and there should be a unique assignment for *each* case.

As noted in Chapter 4, the HORG classification has problems here. The set of rules elaborated by the OPCS for assigning a woman to a category in the SCS varies according to her formal marital status. Thus:

1. when married and living with a spouse the woman is classified on the basis of her husband;
2. when not living with a spouse and in employment the woman is classified on the basis of her own occupation;
3. when not living with a spouse and unemployed, it rather depends...

The convolutions become impenetrable when attempting to classify the single, never-employed woman, who lives on her own and who does not remember her father.

In order to come close to providing a unique assignment for each case, the SCS abandons any pretence of having a uniform basis for classification. A woman may be classified either by her own occupation or by that of any near male relative. This is absurd as well as sexist. If a classification does anything, it ought to group together things (in this case, people) that share some definite and defined characteristics. It is, therefore, rather economical with the truth to say the HORG/SCS provides an exhaustive as well as a unique classification, since these attributes are only achieved at the expense of the only rationale for classifying anything.

6.1.3 A Viable Index

Finally, there are three practical considerations which are important in conducting empirical research and designing tests of hypotheses.

First, it should be easy to *collect the information* on which to base the classification. As anyone with experience of survey research knows, it is often very difficult to elicit unambiguous occupational data from respondents, apart from those who are in regular, fixed employment. To obtain even half-reliable data the interviewer needs to have received some minimal training. The use by the OPCS in classifications of national data on, for example, perinatal mortality only gives the SCS/HORG a spurious exactitude. (Note, however, that many of the other possible options require even more complex information at source.)

Second, there is the issue of the *level of measurement* used. Depending on one's theoretical notion of classness, the appropriate index should be categorical or continuous. A Marxist analysing class structure would not be interested in an index based on a continuous measure such as income, even if grouped into quintiles; a Weberian analysing graduations in prestige would not be interested in a categorical index such as tenure.

Whatever the theoretical framework adhered to by the OPCS, the SCS at best – when every male can be classified – satisfies the requirements, of an ordinal scale; for women, it can never be 'better' than a nominal classification. Indeed, many of the alternatives proposed, such as the various prestige scales (see Hall and Jones, 1953; Hope and Goldthorpe, 1974), have been designed for precisely this reason (see also Oldman and Illsley, 1966).

Third, an indicator should be *sensitive*. If someone's classification according to an index changes, it is obviously important that this change can be related to a change in that person's position in the social hierarchy, to which the classification refers. Goldthorpe (1984) correctly deploys this argument against the use of women's own occupation because married women might change their job for life-cycle reasons unrelated to any change in their social position. It is unrealistic to be rigorous here – if a perfect index existed somewhere we would not be writing this tome – but it is reasonable to demand that the index be relatively sensitive to 'real' change and relatively stable when there is no 'real' change.

The problem is that, if the index has not been derived theoretically, then, when the classification changes – because a person has changed his or her occupation – this could either reflect 'real' change in social position or a property of the indicator. As there is no theory behind the SCS, *post hoc* 'explanations' of funny results abound.

Thus, whilst the conceptual and technical difficulties discussed above are serious and cannot be discussed lightly as several commentators in the 'inequalities of health' debate have done (see, for example, Hart, 1986; Scott-Samuel, 1986; and Wilkinson, 1986), it is perhaps more damning simply to say that the use of the SCS when analysing occupational mortality tables gives peculiar results. For example, the standardised mortality ratio (SMR) of commercial artists (occupation unit 020.21) is 107, whilst that of industrial designers (occupation unit 020.22) is 54. This is not just a question of small numbers. The SMRs of foremen responsible for product inspection and packing (occupation group 136) is 160 (based on 813 deaths) and that of industrial inspectors (occupational group 137) is only 71 (based on 3514 deaths).

6.1.4 A Desirable Index

We have discussed several 'methodological' reasons why the SCS is not very appropriate and how the version used for women, SCS/HORG, is especially unsatisfactory. But complaining about the inadequacy of the SCS is the British sociologists' national pastime (like complaining about the weather, knowing that we can do nothing about it except emigrate). As an empirical instrument HORG can only be properly evaluated in any specific context as 'poor' in comparison to practicable alternatives.

The question, therefore, is whether we can identify an option which:

1. is not circular or prone to misinterpretation or reification;
2. provides a uniform basis for a unique assignment for each case;
3. can be derived from easily collectable data in a form which corresponds to the underlying data phenomenon;
4. is relatively sensitive to changes or stability in the underlying phenomenon.

Ideally, of course, indices should be theoretically based: they should relate to the specified phenomena they indicate in specified ways. However, the debate here has to do with the empirical properties of the classification. For the purposes of a methodological comparison with the SCS, it is more important that the alternative index meet these taxonomic requirements than that it be theoretically justified. We should emphasise that these requirements have not been invented solely to justify our choice below, but are derived from classical arguments about the nature of classification (see Harre, 1964).

6.2 THE OPTIONS

One alternative to the SCS are the prestige scales which have been elaborated on both sides of the Atlantic since the Second World War (for example, the Hall-Jones scale, the Ohlin Wright scale (1978), Duncan's socio-economic classification (1966), or the Hope–Goldthorpe (1974) scale. Some authors argue that prestige scales are inappropriate because 'classness' is categorical rather than continuous. This is a serious theoretical issue but, as we are concerned with portraying gradients in outcomes, the underlying phenomenon is being treated as hierarchical so that prestige scales cannot be ruled out on this basis in this context. Indeed, they may well be useful in theoretical debate and in the study of (the links between) occupational and social stratification; but their occupational basis lays them open to the criticisms that they are increasingly irrelevant (and transient) as indicators of classness for a substantial proportion of the population; and they are even more complicated to use *in practice*, than the SCS. In any case, in our data, this option was not available to us.

We *could* have used the woman's own pre-marital occupation consistently regardless of marital status: we decided against this because it carries many of the same problems as the SCS and observations about the (lack of) salience of pre-marital occupation for many women are persuasive (see above, Chapter 4).

Other proposals abandon the occupational basis of a classification and look for other indices which are supposed to reflect socio-economic status more directly. Our search is, of course, limited by the data available to us, and it is also, to be honest, guided by a desire to provoke, shock and, ideally, titillate.

Three possible candidates are indices based on educational attainment and/or housing tenure and/or income. All three are interesting and have been used in several studies. None of them is circular. They are, of course, prone to misinterpretation and reification if carelessly used, but these problems are easier to avoid than with SCS.

The problem is with the remaining criteria advanced above. Whilst both current housing tenure status and current income provide a uniform basis for an exhaustive and unique assignment, the current educational attainment of an individual varies according to the system which was in force when they were young. One could create equivalence scales but they would be as open to criticism as the HORG scheme.

Data can be collected for two of these three relatively easily. Data can be collected for educational attainment and housing tenure with crude metrics such as number of years of full-time schooling or whether or not owner-occupier/council tenant/other. But the distribution of people in these metrics is very lumpy and not very useful for discriminating; the interpretation of 'years of schooling' varies by age/cohort; the ordering of the tenure classification is debatable; and in both cases, it is not obvious how to develop a finer classification in a unique fashion. In contrast, income provides a unique assignment and can clearly be ordered, but it is difficult to collect reliable data on either household or individual income.

In respect of the criteria of relative sensitivity, educational attainment hardly changes after early adulthood, whilst housing tenure shifts not only with the person's career but also with the pattern of the housing market, and income is also very variable. For the purposes of contrasting with HORG/SCS, this makes educational attainment more interesting but does not exclude the others.

Moreover, we want to emphasise that this book is *not* about proposing *any specific* alternative to the SCS. Our interest in this field started because we were faced with problems – (deceptively?) similar to those of Stevenson – about how best to classify women in order to analyse the distribution of pregnancy-related outcomes in a large data base spanning 30 years. This cast the problems with SCS/HORG in a peculiarly sharp light because of the large shifts in occupational structure and opportunity both for men and for women over that period. But that problem – of considerable shifts in social meaning – also applies to any other obvious choices, such as level of education or housing tenure (although hardly at all to income).

The only remaining candidate in our original data set which has sometimes been related to socio-economic status is the woman's own height. As a classificatory variable it has several advantages:

1. whilst subject to some measurement error, this is small and can eventually be controlled in a careful study;
2. it was available for all subjects in our primary data base;
3. it forms a natural scale and indeed is, more or less, normally distributed.

A priori, of course, it looks very strange to use maternal height an an index for social class. But our purpose in choosing maternal height is expository and methodological: we wish to highlight the methodological characteristics of SCS/HORG as well as the methodological criteria which any index must satisfy, without entering into a debate about the substance of the explanations provided by different indices. For the purposes of a comparative assessment of the empirical properties of HORG/SCS as an index, maternal height is very satisfactory.

In terms of the taxonomic requirements elaborated earlier in the chapter, maternal height is clearly not circular and it is unlikely to be reified; it provides a unique assignment: it is exhaustive; and it is statistically tractable, so that it easily satisfies four of the criteria. In respect of the other two – its explanatory status and its sensitivity to change in status – height is not ideal.

In the former case, maternal height clearly is related physiologically to some of the relevant pregnancy-related outcomes, so that it is an 'impure' index in the sense discussed above (see section 6.1.1). However, whilst we expect maternal height to discriminate pregancy-related outcomes such as birthweight, neo-natal morbidity and perinatal death for physiological reasons, there is no physiological process by which it can affect *fertility* or *fertility-related* outcomes or any other outcomes during development. If one were interested in searching for an explanation, one could proceed in an analogous way to Stevenson, who compared mortality of spouses with that of their husbands in order to isolate the pure social class effect of his occupationally-based scheme. One could compare the power of maternal height in discriminating *pregnancy-related* outcomes with its power in discriminating other outcomes and so obtain an estimate of the 'pure' effect of height as an *index* of 'social classness' over and above its physiological impact, if any. But the purpose of this exercise is different: it is to compare the performance of the existing SCS with an alternative.

The criterion of sensitivity proves rather more of a problem. In contrast to the SCS which, as an indicator, changes (often randomly) for an individual – and so was objected to above on that count – the mother's height does not change at all after adolescence until middle age. If we were studying the pregnancy careers of mothers or other intragenerational processes, this would be a severe disadvantage as it would imply that the underlying social variable which affected life chances did not change through a person's adult life. In fact, the majority of our initial studies were limited to primigravidae and, in addition to the fact that the first birth usually occurs early on in the career of an adult female – and so not long after she attains her adult height – this means that we were *not* concerned with comparisons over time for the same woman.

Whilst, therefore, this was not a problem for our particular set of analyses, this restriction must be acknowledged when we introduce analyses involving other data sets.

6.3 HEIGHT, FERTILITY AND INFANT MORTALITY

Moreover we want to suggest that, if height data had been available to Stevenson, then on the 'official' version of his task (Leete and Fox, 1977), a less concerned statistician may well have been tempted to use height as a discriminator on empirical and practical grounds,[1] rather than to develop from scratch a relatively complex occupationally-based scheme; for if one reflects – superficially – on Stevenson's task, it was to find a variable which would account for differences in fertility and infant mortality.

Of course, the exact form of his argument – that the total fertility to different social classes depends upon when women start their reproductive career and how efficient they are at reproducing – no longer applies with contraception more or less freely available. But, if we were to pursue the task analogous to Stevenson's, then we would also want to examine a social determinant of total fertility and a measure of reproductive outcome. The former can be analysed in our data in terms of the age at first birth, which indeed corresponds to one of Stevenson's own arguments (see Chapter 2, above). For the latter, we have used prematurity which is now commonly acknowledged as a purer measure of reproductive efficiency than infant mortality itself (see Macfarlane and Mugford, 1984).

The data is drawn from the AMNDB (see Chapter 7) and we show only the results for 1976–80. The data collected in Aberdeen cannot be used to produce an exact correspondence to the HORG classification but, because these data refer predominantly to women aged 20–30 (primigravidae), the majority have an attendant male to provide the variable 'social class of husband or putative father' which is the only coherent interpretation of the HORG scheme (see section 6.1 above) and covers about 90 percent of the population.

Table 6.1 shows that there is a relatively strong relationship between the mother's age at first birth and husband's social class, and a weaker one with mother's height. This remains true when the data are restricted to women of a particular educational level. Table 6.2 shows that there are strong relationships between prematurity and both husband's social class and mother's height.

This tabulation makes it clear that the potential of HORG to discriminate these particular variables is restricted to those who declare a spouse's occupation. Within that group HORG does reasonably well, although not as well as maternal height when considering perinatal deaths. But where the concern is with *all* fertility and *all* neo-natal deaths, then the erratic behaviour of the 'excluded' occupational group makes it difficult to interpret the distribution coherently.

Classification Using HORG and the Alternative 65

Table 6.1 Age at first birth by pure husband's social class by woman's own height

Height	Husband's Social class				Not classified	Sample percentage	N
	I + II	IIIN	IIIM	IV + V			
Tallest	26.7	26.1	23.6	22.9	21.6	24.4	1 004
Above average	23.0	24.3	22.8	22.4	21.4	23.3	1 452
Below average	25.9	25.8	22.6	21.7	20.3	22.9	1 550
Smallest	25.5	24.1	22.3	21.8	20.0	22.5	1 028
Total Sample percentage	26.1	24.8	22.8	22.1	20.7		
N	1 081	433	1 562	1 317	641		N = 5 034

Table 6.2 Percentage of pre-maturity: by mothers' height and by husbands' social class 1976–80

Height	Husband's social class					Total sample percentage
	I + II	IIIN	IIIM	IV + V	Unassigned	
Tallest	4.9 (325)	6.3 (63)	8.0 (263)	4.9 (264)	6.0 (33)	5.9 (948)
Above average	3.6 (561)	5.6 (177)	5.5 (799)	8.4 (833)	7.0 (91)	6.1 (2 461)
Below average	6.3 (631)	5.5 (237)	5.7 (1 104)	8.3 (1 191)	9.0 (132)	6.9 (3 295)
Smallest	4.0 (246)	5.7 (122)	7.2 (641)	8.1 (835)	11.0 (102)	7.3 (1 946)
Total sample percentage	4.9 (1 763)	5.7 (599)	6.2 (2 807)	8.0 (3 123)	9.0 (358)	6.7 (8 650)

Note: Sample size in parentheses.

This demonstration of the potential value of maternal height is, of course, restricted only to fertility and infant mortality. Whilst these analyses were included partly for historical purposes, it is not obvious exactly which outcome measures should be used so as to test the empirical efficacy of the social class index. That is the subject of the next chapter.

Note

1. Assuming, however, that Szreter (1984) is right that Stevenson was more concerned to engage a debate with the geneticists, it seems unlikely that he would have used a variable which – at that time – was almost entirely appropriated by the geneticists.

7 Measuring Female Life Chances: The Variables and the Data

The previous chapter showed how maternal height performed rather well in comparison to HORG at discriminating fertility and perinatal outcomes. Whilst that demonstration is interesting, the empirical argument for using and retaining the SCS as a classifier which discriminates is, of course, far more broad. Thus, the SCS has been used to discriminate not only fertility and infant mortality, but also a wide range of death and ill-health variables (see the excellent summary provided in the Black Report (publicly available earlier, Townsend and Davidson 1982); and the update by Whitehead (1987) for the Health Education Council), educational outcomes (Plowden, 1967) and habitual behaviours such as alcohol and tobacco consumption (Cox, Blaxter and Buckle *et al.*, 1984). An illustration of the eclecticism of the measure is the compendium of social class differences edited by Reid and Wormald (1982).

7.1 WHAT KIND OF OUTCOME MEASURES ARE APPROPRIATE?

There is a disturbing lack of clarity in defining the range of outcomes over which an index of social class *should* provide discrimination. Clearly, as the SCS in this context is being used as an indicator of social classness, then, inasmuch as social status – or social class – is valued, the SCS *should* discriminate *social* life chance. But readers would probably think we were wasting their time if we were to present a tabulation of social status – probably measured in terms of social class – by the SCS. Beyond that, the issue seems to be treated empirically in the sense that when SCS/HORG *does* discriminate a condition or outcome it is taken as confirmation of its appropriateness (for example, McDowell, 1981), and when HORG fails to discriminate what might otherwise be thought of as an important measure of status then the tendency is to argue either that social classness does not discriminate that condition (for example, dieting or drinking) of that there is a problem in using the SCS in that particular situation (rate of divorce or single parenthood).

The important point is that this empirical debate is the wrong way round. Consider, for example, the debate as to which of M1, M2 or M3 are better indicators of money supply. The crucial issue is which one performs best in monitoring vital functions of the economy and, whilst the question might be phrased in terms of the appropriateness of M1, M2 or M3, the heated arguments are over which of these functions are more vital than others. Similarly, the point here is to start *not* with the index and then find out empirically whether or not it discriminates between an arbitrary set of valued outcomes, but to *start* by deciding upon the set of valued outcomes and then find out about their social distribution according to a variety of indices.

Of course, the difference between the debate about the validity of indices of money supply and of social class is that (except for a few fanatics) M1, M2 and M3 are *only* indices and not of importance in their own right, whilst nearly everyone is concerned with their social status (which is what they think the SCS measures). It *is one* of the valued outcomes. Because most people value social status itself, they are concerned with their own position on the social class ladder (or one of many ladder; see Young, and Willmott, 1956). The merits of rival indices tend therefore to be debated as if they directly reflected social status.

However, this is only because social status (as measured by social class) is *assumed* to be related to a whole range of other valued outcomes. Recent published debate about the validity of the SCS has concentrated on the portrayal of inequalities in life chances as measured by death rates according to lifetime occupation (Illsley, 1986). It is, of course, recognised that the chance of death is only one – though very important – component of life chances and, within that (belated) debate, more attention has been given recently to social inequalities in *health* (see Blaxter, 1986; Hart, 1986; Carr-Hill, 1987). However, as occupational class performs less well at discriminating 'outcomes'; measures such as health service use – especially for women (see Cartwright and Anderson, 1981) – those authors concerned to portray wide class differentials tend to concentrate on mortality rates.

The demonstration that 'occupational class' does not work very well in a certain context or is counter-intuitive ought to concern proponents of that index but is not a definitive refutation of its value. We have to provide a test: not only in terms of the relative *power* of indices in discriminating a *specific* outcome (like death) but also in terms of the range of valued outcomes which can be discriminated by each of the different indices. To do this we need to known what an index of social status is meant to be discriminating before judging whether a proposed index is or is not adequate. In other words, the objective of the proposed index should be clarified: what are the (female) life chances between which an index of social status should be capable of discriminating?

In general, stratification theorists would expect their social-class index to discriminate power, prestige and wealth. In a 'just', though unequal, society, there is no *theoretical* reason why social classness should distinguish between the average *life expectancies* of different groups, the *access* of their children to education, the availability of *adequate* housing and other 'socially necessary minima' for citizenship (Mack and Lansley, 1987). In 'modern industrialised societies', however, social status tends to discriminate not only power, prestige and wealth but nearly every other component of basic needs (including life expectancy, access to education and adequate housing). According to custom, practice and, sadly, reality, the social class measure is therefore expected to discriminate nearly nearly all elements of the good life.

7.2 MEASURING THE GOOD LIFE

Most recent discussions of how to measure the quality of life (OECD, 1976; Miles, 1985) would include not only healthfulness of life but also other aspects of human development such as attained knowledge, the quality of human activities and of their environment, freedom, human rights and justice. Those discussions have been general – unspecific to gender or to national context – but here an attempt is made to draw up a series of criterial or outcome measures which are appropriate for adult women in post-war British society. By 'appropriate', we mean a set of measures which not only reflects the quality of life which they lead but also where we would be concerned if the quality of life so measured were socially differentiated.

The general scope of quality of life measures includes attained knowledge, the quality of human activities and of their environment, freedom, human rights and justice. But a practical specification for adults in post-war British society ought also to include the prospects for satisfying/happy social relationships with another adult; and, where there are children, that they are themselves healthy and have good life chances. Parsons (1956) might argue that these considerations are only pertinent/relevant for women, but we would argue that this is either gratuitiously sexist or wrong.

These arguments suggest that we should search for indices of all these various measures. To repeat the conclusion of the previous section: we realise that this approach will appear a little curious to those who are *only* concerned, say, with class differences in mortality, or *only* concerned with class differences in educational attainment, and so on. But, in fact, the attraction and, indeed, the hegemony of the occupationally-based social class classification is that it *does* differentiate across a *wide* range of valued outcomes.

Our approach, therefore, is to specify which kinds of outcomes *should* be of interest in assessing female life chances. We have explicitly devalued some (for example, own income above a certain minimum) and emphasised others (for example, the health of their children). Whilst our particular choices may be seen as contentious, the methodological issue here is the breadth of the range of outcome measures which should be considered.

Indeed, ideally, we would be presenting to the reader many more tables in the following chapters. But we are obviously limited by the data available to us and this is taken into account in the discussion below before choosing a set of indicators for the 'good life' which will shape the material presented in Chapter 8.

7.3 THE DATA AVAILABLE

Essentially, apart from secondary analysis of national data, this study is drawn on data collected during the lifetime of the MRC Medical Sociology Unit whilst at Aberdeen. There are two main sources: first, the AMNDB which, for all pregnancies occurring within Aberdeen District, contains social and demographic information (as well as the usual medical data) from 1950 to 1982. This 'Data Bank' is described fully in Samphier and Thompson, (1982).

Second, we have drawn on the Aberdeen Child Development Survey (the 'Reading Survey') which was comprehensive survey of all 7 year olds, 9 year olds and 11 year olds attending primary school in 1961 with a follow-up survey in 1965. Besides the crucial socio-demographic characteristics, information was collected on friendship networks, the home environment and the results of a wide range of psychomotor tests. This survey is described fully in Illsley and Carr-Hill (forthcoming).

Other sources which will be used are: supplementary data collected in 1951, 1961, 1971 and 1981 (the 'Census' data) on 50 percent of the primiparae in those years concerned with their housing and the condition of the neonate; and also the Low Birth Weight study (LBW data) of all low birthweight children born in 1970, together with an equal number of matched controls who were followed up 10 years later. The study is described fully in Illsley and Mitchell (1984).

Where appropriate, we shall also be drawing on two national sources: first, a survey carried out by the OPCS of adult heights and weights

(Knight, 1984). The survey was a cross-sectional random sample of 10 363 adults in the United Kingdom in August and September 1980. Respondents were measured in their homes by trained interviewers. Second, we shall also be using the Health and Lifestyle Survey (henceforth HALS): a nationally representative survey of 8500 adults in Great Britain carried out in 1984. The survey covered both self-report and physiological data: subjects were interviewed and measured in their own homes.

Finally, we shall also include some material from the most recent follow-up to the households of the children of those interviewed by Seebohm Rowntree in York in 1950 (see Carr-Hill, 1986). Whilst the 1880 individuals for whom there is data are not a proper sample of any conceivable population, it includes material not available elsewhere.

7.4 VARIABLES AND DATA FOR QUALITY OF LIFE INDICATORS

7.4.1 Health

Obviously, the crucial measure remains life expectancy. That said, it is very difficult to reach agreement as to how 'healthfulness' should be measured. A wide variety of indices has been proposed to measure positive health, minor morbidity and serious morbidity, but there is little agreement (see Carr-Hill, 1983). In the AMNDB we are limited to the blood pressures of pregnant women. In the other studies a much wider range of health data is available on both clinical health status measures and on self-reported health scales.

7.4.2 Attained Knowledge

Without a basic level of knowledge and awareness of the mores of the society in which one finds oneself, it is impossible to act autonomously within that society. At the same time, there is also the perspective of knowledge being one of the higher ends of human existence.

The emphasis ought to be on what is actually learnt by individuals without assuming that this necessarily corresponds to the length of time being educated. Nevertheless the only (rather poor) data available to most researcher is the number of years of completed full-time schooling and the level of formal qualification obtained and that is what has been used in this study. It would have been possible to use slightly more sophisticated measures in the National Child Development Survey but it would have added little to the argument.

7.4.3 Human Activities

What people do – their activities – has long been regarded as a major aspect of well-being. On a philosophical level, it can be argued that 'people are what they do' and, if we consider particular categories of human activity, social scientists, (not to mention individuals themselves) have long regarded paid employment as one key determinant of well-being or lack of it. Recently, 'leisure' has been of increasing interest as a source of their emancipation or passive boredom, and the present-day feminist movement has draw attention to the importance of a third major category: housework and child care.

There are a number of ways in which human activities can be evaluated:

1. the way people spend their time;
2. the quality of activities themselves;
3. the social aspects of activities;
4. the productiveness of activities;
5. the access to activities (see Carr-Hill and Lintott, 1986).

Our data do not permit such sophistication; on the other hand given the arguments in Chapters 4 and 5 above, it is not appropriate to use the 'obvious' marker for the 'quality' of human activities in the current social configuration, i.e. occupational status. For these reasons, breakdowns of this aspect are *not* included. However, some illustrative 'health-behaviour' type data are available and these have been analysed.

7.4.4 Material Possessions

The problem here is to develop criteria of what goods, individually or collectively consumed, really do contribute to well-being. Access to a minimum of certain goods is essential for the satisfaction of basic needs: food, water, clothing, shelter and sanitation. Furthermore, the concern is not only with strict minima but with the quality of these goods.

Given the overall argument of the book about the difficulty of measuring social status we have to be careful in our interpretation of the analysis. Here, we simply record that both in the Data Bank and in the Reading Survey we have available locally derived classifications of the mother's pre-marital occupations, her father's, and her husband's occupation as well as the SCS classification of her husband.

Once again our Aberdeen data in this respect is very limited: we are only able to consider the rateable value of the house in different Census years.

Measuring Life Chances: Variables and Data 73

However, in some other studies, questions were asked about consumer durables.

7.4.5 Relating

There are convincing reasons for regarding how people relate to each other as a fundamental aspect of their well-being. Some might argue that this is even more important with the adult women who are the subjects of this study. Data in this area is, however, sparse and subject to clear biases both in construction and reporting (why is sitting in a pub more superficial than going to the opera?). We have, therefore, only considered a limited range of 'outcomes' of relationships; specifically the percentages of teenage first births and of prenuptial conceptions. Clearly, these can be interpreted both way but they, at least, are reasonable objective data.

7.4.6 A Happy Family

The argument here is that one important aspect of the adult quality of life is the development and opportunities available to their progeny. This is a departure from the relatively simple structure of outcome measures above, which were all individually based. It is clear, however, that the children's welfare is of crucial interest to their parents and forms part of their own welfare as perceived by the parents themselves.

One could repeat a whole series of similar measures relative to the children, but there is surely a limit to the parent's legitimate interest in the development of their children: the child must have the freedom to determine her own destiny (United Nations, 1989). Instead, the concern should be restricted to the *opportunities* for the healthy mental and physical development of their children. This suggests concentration on: (i) indicators of physical development such as birthweight and height adjusted for age; (ii) indicators of mental development such as IQ and other test scores. Some data for these are available in the Reading Survey.

7.5 THE EMPIRICAL COMPARISON OF DISCRIMINATION

In the next chapter, therefore, we compare the relative performance of SCS/HORG and maternal height in discriminating female life chances along the dimensions detailed above. This will be done very simply without taking into account any of the (obvious) interrelationships and confounding factors. The intention is not to construct a validated model to explain disparities but, much more modestly, to assess which of the indices provides a better picture of the pattern.

Finally, there is the question of *how* it should discriminate: in terms of which index of measure of association. Thus the classic presentation in terms of the SCS – or indeed any other categorical scheme – is with a cross-tabulation showing the average or proportion in each of the categories of the Scheme. But, of course, the presentation is constrained to this form by the fact that the SCS is a categorical variable in the first place. When using SCS in a multivariate context one is usually further constrained to treat the SCS variable (or equivalents) as a factor with no implied ordering at all (for a bizarre exception see Dowding, 1981). Moreover, in that mode, the categorical variable has to be treated as if each level of the factor corresponds to a dummy sub-variable so that the 'effect of social class' is in fact analysed in terms of a set of sub-variables, which is not quite the same thing.

A variable such as maternal height, however, has many other possibilities. First, it can be treated, as it is, as a continuous interval-level variable. In this mode, it has the extra advantage of being (probably) normally distributed. Or it can be split into categories – for example, quartiles – which, by definition, are ordered from short to tall.

In order to compare directly with SCS, we have, in the Aberdeen data, adopted a fourfold division of heights at 153.5, 159.5 and 164.5 which splits the distribution, roughly, into quartiles; in using the HALS data, the corresponding divisions are 156, 160.5 and 165 reflecting the welfare improvements in the 1950s and 1960s; and so on. We have also checked the comparative performance of maternal height and SCS in a regression context by using four dummy variables for each of the four categories of SCS. Whilst SCS nearly always outperforms height, it should be emphasised that the SCS factor is associated with four degrees of freedom whilst the maternal height variable only corresponds to one; moreover there remains the problem of unassigned cases.

8 The Distribution of Female Life Chances

8.1 INTRODUCTION

The purpose of this chapter is to examine empirically the final justification of the HORG classification: that it works. This is, essentially, a methodological exercise assessing the usefulness of HORG in discriminating between valued outcomes for women. Because this is an empirical issue, we have to make this assessment in comparison to some other possible index and we have suggested using the woman's own height as one which fulfils several of the technical criteria for a reliable and useful index (and certainly more so than HORG).

At the same time, we have shown that, when used for women, the HORG classification (the occupation of the head of household) usually involves classifying women by their husband's occupation, sometimes by their own, occasionally by their father's occupation, and very occasionally by someone else's altogether. This is obviously very untidy; it is very difficult to interpret a table showing variation in outcomes for women by an (occupationally-based) social class classification.

It should be noted, however, that the current justification for using HORG (compare Goldthorpe, 1983 and 1984) rests on the male's greater commitment to or continuity in the labour market precisely because, *in practice,* HORG usually involves classifying women by their husband's occupation. For this reason, in order to assess whether the extra complication of using HORG actually improves the discriminatory power, we have also presented data (where possible) using a 'pure' husband's social class index (occupationally-based).

In the next section of this chapter, therefore, we compare the distribution of various measures of female life chances according to, separately, the HORG classification based primarily on the husband's occupation, women's own height and, where possible, a 'pure' husband's social class classification. The various dimensions which will be taken to reflect the range of female life chances – across which an index should 'work' – have been discussed in the previous chapter. We suggested that five aspects should be taken into account: health, learning, material possessions, opportunities for work and leisure, relating and prognosis for a happy family life.

In making our assessment of the utility of HORG relative to a pure husband's social class and the woman's own height, we shall be focusing on two issues: first, the exhaustiveness of the classification. It became clear from the preliminary analyses reported in Chapter 6 that the smoothness of the gradient varied according to whether or not women without a husband were 'simply' excluded from the analysis or treated as an extra undifferentiated social group of 'unknowns'. Likewise, the height variable can be grouped into four or five categories, or treated correctly as a continuous variable. All possible combinations have been attempted and, whilst only some have been reported, commentary is included on any substantial variations.

Similarly, in most cases, only the distributions with each of the 'test' classifiers are presented. But one of the desiderata of a classifier is that it should also discriminate within sub-groups of the population. We have, therefore, also presented some tables showing cross-tabulations of a criterion by both height and HORG.

Second, one of the justifications often advanced for retaining a classification or index based on a particular statistical series (such as the OPCS occupational categories) is that, if the basis of classification is radically changed. then 'we lose continuity' (see Chapter 3). Similar remarks are made about HORG. Of course, this justification only works if other conditions also remain the same. Given that we are assessing the empirical properties of HORG, we have therefore also examined how the gradients/patterns displayed by HORG and by women's height have changed over the period since the Second World War.

Our ability to carry out an 'ideal' set of comparisons for the assessment is, of course, constrained by the available data. The data sets available to us were also described in the previous chapter and it can be seen that, in consequence, the analyses below tend to emphasise health-related outcome variables. The importance of this limitation will be taken up in the concluding chapter.

The data are presented with a bare minimum of commentary, although we recognise that some of the tables are substantively interesting in their own right. Finally, we have preferred to present all the relevant data before making an overall commentary on the adequacy of the indices as discriminators in Part III.

8.2 CONTEMPORARY DATA ON HEALTH

Three kinds of data are considered here: self-reports of health and level of

The Distribution of Female Life Chances

disability; various physiological measures; and results on scales of psychological distress.

8.2.1 Self-Reported Health

Whilst they are very general, the basic questions included in the General Household Survey (GHS) have been shown to 'correlate very well with health assessed in more objective ways (Cox, Blaxter, Buckle et al. 1987, p. 2).

The data in Table 8.1 show a gradient with social class with values for the unassigned hovering somewhere in the middle and only a very weak gradient with height. However, the other main question from the GHS ('Have you any long standing disability, illness or infirmity?') shows a weak gradient by HORG with the unassigned reporting most illness, a clear gradient by husband's social class with the unassigned in the middle and, once again, a weak one by height (see Table 8.2).

In contrast, one of the scales which is used quite widely, the Nottingham Health Profile, shows a gradient by both height and social class, although the gradient is stronger by height than by social class (see Table 8.3).

Table 8.1 Percentage reporting poor health (overall mean: 28.6, N = 5077)

	Husband's social class					
Height (cm)	I + II	IIIN	IIIM	IV + V	Unassigned	All
165 and up	20.7	27.5	28.7	38.4	24.0	28.0
	(584)	(368)	(588)	(401)	(50)	(1 991)
160.6–165	17.0	25.4	29.6	34.1	27.3	25.0
	(324)	(142)	(351)	(208)	(22)	(1 047)
156–160.5	21.3	32.7	29.3	35.1	56.3	29.3
	(272)	(150)	(341)	(214)	(16)	(993)
Up to 156	23.6	28.2	34.5	36.5	30.8	31.7
	(229)	(131)	(383)	(277)	(26)	(1 046)
All	20.4	28.2	30.4	36.4	30.7	28.6
	(1 409)	(791)	(1 663)	(1 100)	(114)	(5 077)

Source: HALS; authors' own calculations.

Table 8.2 Percentage reporting disability (the GHS question) broken down by test indices

	Social class of head of household (HORG)		Husband's social class or no husband		Own height	
I + II	17.1	(1 185)	18.0	(898)	Tall	19.3 (1 363)
IIIN	23.2	(629)	20.8	(375)	Above average	20.8 (1 247)
IIIM	20.1	(1 881)	21.8	(1 513)	Below average	19.7 (1 283)
IV + V	23.1	(940)	22.4	(610)	Short	24.6 (1 307)
Unassigned	30.7	(407)	21.8	(1 682)	–	–
	21.2	(5 042)	21.1	(5 078)		21.1 (5 200)

Source: Authors' calculations from Knight (1984).

Table 8.3 Percentage of population giving positive Nottingham Health Profile NHP score

	Husband's social class					
Height	I + II	IIIN	IIIM	IV + V	Unassigned	All
Tallest	9 (43)	9 (32)	3 (68)	14 (29)	25 (8)	8 (180)
Above average	18 (33)	19 (59)	21 (58)	16 (38)	31 (16)	20 (204)
Below average	12 (25)	24 (97)	29 (38)	25 (59)	30 (10)	24 (229)
Smallest	31 (16)	11 (44)	37 (27)	28 (36)	55 (11)	27 (134)
All	15 (117)	18 (232)	18 (191)	22 (162)	36 (45)	20 (747)

Note: Sample size in parentheses.
Source: Carr-Hill (1987).

8.2.2 Physiological Measures

Two kinds of data are considered here: records of blood pressure monitored during first pregnancies in Aberdeen in 1976–8; and one perinatal outcome often considered to reflect the mother's physical condition.

8.2.2.1 Blood Pressure Levels

One aspect of a mother's health is the likelihoood of pre-eclampsia during pregnancy. Table 8.4 shows the incidence of pre-eclampsia in cells defined by mother's height and husband's social class. It has been suggested (Butler and Alberman, 1969) that there is a U-shaped relation between social class and pre-eclampsia, but it can be seen that there is very little relation in these data and this is also true for tables broken down by educational level.

8.2.2.2 Birth Outcomes

As an index of maternal health, we present the likelihood of prematurity among primaparae (see also Table 6.2). Table 8.5 shows how the proportion

Table 8.4 Percentage of pre-eclampsia* broken down by mother's height and by husband's social class 1976–80

		\multicolumn{6}{c}{Husband's social class}				
		I + II	IIIN	IIIM	IV + V	Unassigned	All
	Tallest	35.1	30.2	38.4	36.0	33.0	35.9
		(325)	(63)	(263)	(264)	(33)	(948)
	Above	29.9	31.1	33.4	33.3	35.0	32.5
	average	(561)	(177)	(799)	(833)	(91)	(2 461)
Mother's	Below	31.7	35.9	33.2	33.6	28.0	33.0
height	average	(631)	(237)	(1 104)	(1 191)	(132)	(3 295)
	Smallest	30.1	35.2	34.0	34.6	25.0	33.4
		(246)	(122)	(641)	(835)	(102)	(1 946)
	All	31.5	33.7	33.9	34.0	30.0	33.2
		(1 763)	(599)	(2 807)	(3 123)	(358)	(8 650)

* Pre-eclampsia defined as a diastolic blood pressure reading of 90 mm. hg or more on two consecutive occasions at least 24 hours apart and Esback more than 0.25g/litre.

Note: Sample size in parentheses.
Source: AMNDB.

Table 8.5 Percentage of premature births in Aberdeen, 1976–80, according to test indices

	Husband's social class		Own height		
I + II	4.9	(1 763)	Tall	5.9	(948)
IIIN	5.7	(599)	Above average	6.1	(2 461)
IIIM	6.2	(2 807)	Below average	6.9	(3 295)
IV + V	8.0	(3 123)	Short	7.3	(1 946)
Unassigned	9.0	(358)	–		
	6.7	(8 650)		6.7	(8 650)

Source: AMNDB.

of premature births moves from 4.9 among social classes I and II to 8.0 among social classes IV and V with a rate of 9.0 among the unassigned; and from 5.9 among the tallest women to 7.3 among the shortest women.

8.2.3 Psychological Measures

A wide range of possible measures for psychological distress exist. For the purpose of this analysis, we have concentrated on the one which is most widely used in the UK (the GHS). Table 8.6 shows the distribution according to height and HORG social class in the Rowntree data.

There seems to be no doubt that height is a much more powerful discriminator than HORG social class on these data, with more than twice as many giving a positive response among the smallest compared to the tallest, and with similar gradients occurring within three of the four social class groups. A very similar variable derived from HALS a malaise score produces a similar result (see Table 8.7).

8.3 LEARNING

We have already lamented the lack of good data in this area. Simply for completeness, we have included a breakdown of the percentage who stayed on after the minimum school-leaving age.

Table 8.6 Percentage population giving positive GHQ score

Height	Husband's social class					All
	I + II	IIIN	IIIM	IV + V	Unassigned	
Smallest	50	25	52	33	64	39
	(16)	(44)	(27)	(36)	(11)	(134)
Below average	24	29	32	27	40	29
	(25)	(97)	(38)	(59)	(10)	(229)
Above average	24	25	17	26	25	23
	(33)	(59)	(58)	(38)	(16)	(204)
Highest	14	25	12	17	63	18
	(43)	(32)	(68)	(29)	(8)	(180)
All	24	27	23	27	44	26
	(117)	(232)	(191)	(162)	(45)	(747)

Note: Sample size in parentheses.
Source: Carr-Hill (1987).

Table 8.7 Mean number of reported psycho-social symptoms

Height (cm)	Husband's social class					Total
	I + II	IIIN	IIIM	IV + V	Unassigned	
Up to 156	2.3	2.4	2.6	2.9	2.6	2.6
	(229)	(132)	(384)	(281)	(26)	(1 052)
156–160.5	2.2	2.6	2.3	2.7	3.3	2.4
	(272)	(150)	(342)	(214)	(16)	(994)
160.6–165	2.2	2.5	2.5	2.7	2.7	2.4
	(326)	(142)	(353)	(210)	(22)	(1 053)
165 and up	2.2	2.2	2.3	2.6	2.9	2.3
	(587)	(369)	(588)	(405)	(50)	(1 999)
All	2.2	2.4	2.4	2.7	2.8	2.4
	(1 414)	(793)	(1 667)	(1 110)	(114)	(5 098)

Note: Sample size in parentheses.
Source: HALS.

It is unsurprising to learn from Table 8.8 that there are more than three times as many who move into husband's social class I and II who stayed on at school as those who move into husband's social class IV and V (cf. 77.7 percent and 24.9 percent). It is perhaps less expected that there is also an association between mother's height and the extent of staying on at school.

8.4 MATERIAL POSSESSIONS

There are, of course, a wide number of indices which could have been used here. We have restricted the presentation to those reflecting assets and wealth rather than income because of the difficulty of intrafamily distribution of income.

8.4.1 Rateable Values

It is perhaps unsurprising to find from Table 8.9 that there is a strong association between rateable value and the husband's social class(declining from £252.40 for social classes and II to £193.30 for IV and V) although the unclassifieds (with no husband's occupation recorded) sit unhappily in the upper middle at £226.80. It is much more interesting to record the admittedly smaller increase in mean rateable value from £194.90 among the shortest to £227.60 for the tallest. Moreover, this increasing relationship holds also among those who are *unclassified* by husband's social class.

Table 8.8 Percentage leaving school with no further qualifications by height and HORG

| Height (cm) | Husband's social class | | | | | |
	I + II	IIIN	IIIM	IV + V	Unassigned	All
165 and up	45	59	73	86	62	60
160·6 – 165	40	47	69	72	37	58
156 – 160·5	28	41	67	69	41	51
Up to 156	45	29	56	64	27	54
All	38	43	66	73	43	54

Source: HALS.

The Distribution of Female Life Chances

Table 8.9 Rateable value in 1981 (£) in Aberdeen by test indices of measures of female social class

	Pure husband's HORG social class		Own height		
I + II	252	(113)	Tall	228	(127)
IIIN	226	(53)	Above average	217	(133)
IIIM	187	(165)	Below average	209	(138)
IV + V	193	(136)	Short	195	(148)
Unassigned	227	(79)	–	–	
All	212	(546)		212	(546)

Note: Sample size in parentheses.
Source: AMNDB, Census Years.

In contrast, when we look at tenure status itself in the national survey, the SCS data is clearly superior. Whilst there is a (small) gradient according to mother's height, it is overshadowed by the relationship with SCS (see Table 8.10). Indeed, one is led to suspect that the Registrar-General's classifications are influenced by tenure status rather than vice versa!

8.4.2 Consumer Durables

In the Rowntree Survey, we did ask about the ownership or use of a car, a telephone, a (clothes) washing machine, a dishwasher and a freezer and whether or not the home was centrally heated. The mean numbers in each group are shown in Table 8.11 and there is a clear gradient with husband's social class with the unassigned at the bottom of the heap, but only a very small gradient with height.

8.5 QUALITY OF ACTIVITIES

As explained in Chapter 7 (pp. 00–00), employment and occupational data were not obviously appropriate in this context.. The presentation below is limited, therefore, to 'lifestyle' (expressive consumption) behavioural data. Thus, the proportion who smoke moves from 30.5 percent among women in

Table 8.10 Percentage owner-occupiers (%)

	Social class of head of household (HORG)		Husband's social class or no husband		Own height	
I + II	82.1	(1 205)	87.3	(903)	Tall	65.6 (1 375)
IIIN	67.3	(643)	77.4	(377)	Above average	60.3 (1 258)
IIIM	55.3	(1 911)	57.3	(1 519)	Below average	57.2 (1 297)
IV + V	36.6	(975)	41.7	(618)	Short	50.0 (1 318)
Unassigned	31.5	(412)	43.6	(1 774)	–	–
All	57.6	(5 146)	57.5	(5 191)		58.3 (5 248)

Note: Sample size in parentheses.
Source: Knight (1984).

Table 8.11 Mean number of consumer durables by height and by husband's social class

	Husband's social class (HORG)					
Height	I + II	IIIN	IIIM	IV + V	Unassigned	All
Tallest	3.0	2.8	2.4	1.9	1.9	2.5
Above average	3.0	2.7	2.2	2.1	2.1	2.4
Below average	2.7	2.6	2.2	1.9	1.8	2.3
Smallest	2.9	2.6	1.9	2.1	1.6	2.3
All	2.9	2.6	2.2	2.0	1.9	2.4

Source: Carr-Hill (1987).

husband's social class I and II to 47.9 percent among husband's social class IV and V (see Table 8.12). This is a much stronger relationship than can be observed between mother's height and smoking habits. Both tall women and those in classes I and II tend to slim more frequently than the average:

but the largest difference is between tall and short women (see Table 8.13). Finally, whilst the class gradient for reported alcohol consumption is (almost) upside down, the breakdown by height illustrates geograhically how miniaturisation was a feature of public houses before any other industry (see Table 8.14).

Table 8.12 Smokes now (%)

	Social class of head of household		Pure husband's social class or no husband		Own height		
I + II	30.5	(1 189)	30.3	(899)	Tall	38.4	(1 371)
IIIN	37.5	(632)	35.5	(375)	Above average	40.0	(1 252)
IIIM	40.7	(1 888)	42.2	(1 514)	Below average	39.9	(1 289)
IV + V	47.9	(953)	48.2	(614)	Short	41.4	(1 316)
Unassigned	47.3	(408)	40.4	(1 706)	–	–	
All	39.8	(5 070)	39.7	(5 108)		40.1	(5 228)

Note: Sample size in parentheses.
Source: Knight (1984).

Table 8.13 Slimming (%)

	Social class of head of household		Husband's social class or no husband		Own height		
I + II	31.2	(1 184)	30.2	(896)	Tall	31.7	(1 370)
IIIN	27.4	(631)	27.5	(375)	Above average	30.3	(1 249)
IIIM	31.6	(1 885)	32.6	(1 511)	Below average	31.4	(1 290)
IV + V	27.6	(955)	28.8	(617)	Short	25.7	(1 313)
Unassigned	26.5	(408)	28.0	(1 701)	–	–	
All	29.8	(5 063)	29.8	(5 100)		29.8	(5 222)

Note: Sample size in parentheses.
Source: Knight (1984).

86   Constructing a Social Classification for Women

Table 8.14   Drinks less than once a week (%)

	Social class of head of household		Pure husband's social class or no husband		Own height		
I + II	44.5	(1 205)	42.6	(900)	Tall	51.2	(1 375)
IIIN	56.9	(643)	58.4	(377)	Above average	55.2	(1 258)
IIIM	56.3	(1 911)	57.5	(1 519)	Below average	55.6	(1 297)
IV + V	57.9	(975)	61.6	(618)	Short	59.6	(1 318)
Unassigned	63.6	(412)	54.7	(1 774)	–	–	
All	54.5	(5 146)	54.5	(5 188)		55.3	(5 798)

Note: Sample size in parentheses.
Source: Knight (1984).

8.6 RELATING

The classic index of the breakdown of family life since the Second World War is the 'rising proportion of teenage first births' blamed especially on the lower social classes. The strong relation between husband's social class and the proportion of teenage first births is shown in Table 8.15. The use of mothers' heights also shows a uniform gradient, although not as marked. One might expect that similar relation should be observed with what appears to be a cognate index: the proportion of prenuptial conceptions (that is, legitimate births conceived before marriages). These also follow an interesting pattern (see Table 8.16). First it appears that IIIM were most likely to conceive before marriage in this period, whilst the relationship between mother's height and pre-nuptial conception was more systematic. When the tables are restricted to women of a particular educational level, the relationships are, of course, weakened, but even ignoring the aberrant behaviour of IIIM, there is no obvious relationship between husband's social class and pre-nuptial conception, whilst the trend of decreasing rates of pre-nuptial conception with increasing height is still evident at least among those who stayed on at school.

Table 8.15 Percentage of teenage first births in Aberdeen, 1976–80, according to test indices

	HORG		Husband's social class or no husband		Own height		
I + II	4.1	(1 080)	4.2	(1 081)	Tall	15.0	(1 004)
IIIN	16.5	(562)	6.7	(433)	Above average	19.2	(1 452)
IIIM	19.8	(1 619)	17.9	(1 562)	Below average	22.4	(1 550)
IV + V	33.3	(1 457)	41.6	(1 317)	Short	26.7	(1 028)
Unassigned	34.3	(300)	34.9	(641)	–	–	
All	20.8	(5 018)	20.9	(5 034)		20.9	(5 034)

Note: Sample size in parentheses.
Source: AMNDB.

Table 8.16 Percentage of pre-nuptial conceptions in Aberdeen, 1976–80, according to test indices

	HORG		Own height		
I + II	4.9	(1 763)	Tall	6.9	(948)
IIIN	6.0	(599)	Above average	8.7	(2 461)
IIIM	11.5	(2 807)	Below average	9.8	(3 295)
IV + V	10.1	(3 123)	Short	10.3	(1 946)
Unassigned	11.0	(358)	—		—
All	9.3	(8 650)		9.3	(8 650)

Note: Sample size in parentheses.
Source: AMNDB.

8.7 PROGNOSIS

The difficulty of establishing a coherent set of indication was explained on Chapter 7. The presentation here is limited to two indicators: the rate of low birthweight of children in different groups and the average IQ (from the Reading Survey). The percentage of low birthweight changes similarly from 4.7 among social classes I and II to 9.3 among social classes IV and V, and from 10.0 among the shortest women to 4.5 among the tallest women (see Table 8.17). The relationships hold (more or less) within each category of mother's height and of husband's social class.

The restriction to those of a particular educational level shows how the relationship between husband's social class and percentage of low birthweight is considerably weakened in that none of the rows of either table is monotonic, whilst the relationship between mother's height and the percentage of low birthweight is still quite strong.

Table 8.18 shows the breakdown of recorded IQ according to mother's height and husband's social class from the Reading Survey. There is a clear gradient with social class, the unclassified being at the bottom of the heap; there is a weaker gradient with height.

The case control study of low birthweight children asked a variety of questions about the child-rearing behaviour and expectation of the mothers

Table 8.17 Percentage of low birthweight in Aberdeen, 1976–80, by test indices

	Husband's social class or unassigned		Own height		
I + II	4.7	(1 794)	Tall	4.4	(948)
IIIN	5.5	(605)	Above average	5.6	(2 461)
IIIM	6.9	(2 851)	Below average	7.7	(3 294)
IV + V	9.3	(3 177)	Short	10.1	(1 946)
Unassigned	9.0	(367)	–	–	
All	7.3	(8 794)		7.3	(8 649)

Note: Sample size in parentheses.
Source: AMNDB.

Table 8.18 Average IQ according to husband's social class and mother's height

		Husband's social class				
		I + II	IIIN	IIIM	IV + V	Unassigned	All
	Tall	119.3 (351)	112.2 (199)	109.4 (614)	104.0 (288)	104.0 (68)	110.8 (1 520)
	Medium	117.7 (533)	113.5 (496)	108.8 (1 645)	104.0 (877)	99.8 (219)	109.0 (3 770)
Mother's height	Small	116.2 (452)	112.2 (496)	107.2 (1 862)	101.6 (1 171)	99.5 (277)	106.7 (4 258)
	Short	117.8 (89)	110.3 (144)	105.5 (599)	100.3 (520)	97.5 (138)	104.1 (1 490)
	All	117.6 (1 425)	112.5 (1 335)	107.8 (4 720)	102.3 (2 856)	99.6 (702)	107.7 (11 038)

Note: Sample size in parentheses.
Source: Reading Survey.

of low birthweight children and of the mothers of children in case-control families. Let us first consider the mothers of 'normal' birthweight children. The study (reported in Illsley and Mitchell, 1984) found consistent relationships between husband's social class and indices of mobility and professional status, recreational activity, belief inability to influence development and the interviewer's assessment of the mother. The same pattern of relationships occurs among the parents of low birthweight babies although not at all for the belief in ability to influence development: there are much less consistent relationships with mother's height. However, the only *strong* relationship occurred between husband's social class and the interviewer's assessment of the mother's fluency, logical thought and vocabulary. The breakdowns are presented in Table 8.19: there are gradients with height as with class.

8.8 HISTORICAL DATA ON HEALTH

Whether or not HORG 'works' on current data, it is often said that a classification should be retained because it provides continuity. This is

Table 8.19 Interviewer's assessment of the mother; ratings† of their fluency, logical thought and vocabulary

Husband's social class	Birthweight				Mother's height	Birthweight			
	Normal Rating	N	Low Rating	N		Normal Rating	N	Low Rating	N
I + II	21.7	(22)	21.5	(15)	Tall	17.8	(54)	16.5	(22)
IIIN	19.4	(7)	16.2	(49)	Above average	16.6	(48)	13.3	(39)
IIIM	14.4	(49)	13.2	(43)	Below average	14.5	(10)	13.4	(47)
IV + V	13.3	(53)	11.2	(24)	Short	11.5	(29)	11.7	(23)
All	15.5	(131)	13.6	(131)	All	15.5	(131)	13.6	(131)

Note: Ratings are 131 out of 30; Sample size in parentheses.
Source: Illsley and Mitchell (1984); authors' own calculations.

specious (see Chapter 3 above and compare Goldblatt, 1988) but, in the empirical spirit with which we are assessing the properties of HORG, in the next section we examine the pattern of discrimination provided by HORG over time as compared to that provided by women's height.

The data available for such an examination is, however, extremely limited: the only data set with both height and HORG over a substantial period is the AMNDB.

8.8.1 Pre-Eclampsia

The demonstration above shows that blood pressure varies both by husband's social class and by mother's height. No historical data of this sort is available to us. However, it is possible to compare the breakdown of preeclampsia by husband's social class and mother's height over three periods (see Tables 8.20 and 8.21).

The first point to note is that the rate of pre-eclampsia has increased consistently from 13.8 percent in 1956–60 to 20.9 percent in 1966–70 to 29.2 percent in 1976–80. This steady increase itself says much about the extent to which pre-eclampsia can be taken as a 'solid' measure of physiological condition.

The Distribution of Female Life Chances

Table 8.20 Percentage of moderate or severe pre-eclamptic Toxaemia according to husband's social class in three periods

Period	Hypertension	Unassigned	I + II	IIIN	IIIM	IV + V	Total
1956–60	PET	13.8	17.4	23.1	20.7	17.8	19.7
		(239)	(2 171)	(2 242)	(7 342)	(4 715)	(16 709)
1966–70	PET	20.9	22.7	26.7	23.2	22.2	23.1
		(297)	(2 207)	(1 298)	(5 357)	(4 495)	(13 654)
1976–80	PET	29.2	31.4	34.0	33.89	33.8	33.1
		(367)	(1 795)	(605)	(2 851)	(3 177)	(8 795)

$\chi^2 = 45.2, 11.8, 6.7$; Summary Gamma $= -0.0065$.
Note: Sample sizes in parentheses.
Source: AMNDB.

Table 8.21 Percentage of moderate or severe pre-eclamptic Toxaemia according to mother's height in three periods

Period	Hypertension	Shortest	Small	Medium	Tall	Total
1956–60	PET	18.2	20.3	20.2	21.3	19.7
		(5 161)	(5 702)	(4 486)	(1 276)	(16 625)
1966–70	PET	21.1	23.9	22.9	26.5	23.2
		(3 329)	(5 272)	(3 854)	(1 131)	(13 586)
1976–80	PET	33.4	33.0	32.5	35.9	33.3
		(1 946)	(3 295)	(2 461)	(948)	(8 650)

$\chi^2 = 11.3, 16.9, 3.7$; Summary Gamma $= 0.048$.
Note: Sample size in parentheses.
Source: AMNDB.

The breakdown of social class shows how if even those not assigned to a social class are ignored, there is never a smooth relationship between the proportion of pre-eclampsia and husband's social class. It is interesting to note that those with a husband in low-status non-manual occupations consistently have the highest rate and those in the unassigned group consistently have the lowest rate of pre-eclampsia.

The breakdown by mother's height is of more interest. Thus, in the recent period, there is no discernible relationship between mother's height and the proportion of pre-eclampsia; but both in 1956–60 and 1966–70, it does appear that taller people had higher rates of pre-eclampsia.

8.8.2 Birth Outcomes

Once again, the presentation focuses on the percentage of prematurity. Tables 8.22 and 8.23 present the breakdowns of the percentage of prematurity broken down by husband's social class and by mother's height respectively over the three periods. It can be seen that the overall rates of prematurity have dropped to the present rate of 6.7 percent from about 13 percent in the previous two decades. In particular, whilst the proportions unassigned to any social class have increased substantially (from 1.5 percent to 4.2 percent), their rate of prematurity has dropped from 25.5 percent to 9.0 percent.

The strong association between husband's social class and the proportion of prematurity in 1976–80 is repeated in each of the two previous periods. It is clear that the largest gap is between mothers with husbands in social classes IV and V and the rates in other social classes. If there is a place for the unassigned group, it is beyond social classes IV and V. In contrast, there was a consistent but weak relationship between mother's height and the percentage of prematurity.

Table 8.22 Percentage of premature births according to husband's social class in three periods

Period	Maturity	Husband's social class					
		Unassigned	I + II	IIIN	IIIM	IV + V	Total
1956–60	Prem	25.5	8.7	9.9	11.6	18.6	13.2
		(239)	(2 171)	(2 242)	(7 342)	(4 715)	(16 709)
1966–70	Prem.	15.5	9.2	8.6	11.4	16.9	12.7
		(297)	(2 207)	(1 298)	(5 357)	(4 495)	(13 654)
1976–80	Prem.	9.0	4.9	5.6	6.2	8.0	6.7
		(367)	(1 795)	(605)	(2 851)	(3 177)	(8 795)

χ^2 = 228.8, 126.7, 23.4; Summary Gamma = –0.190.
Note: Sample sizes in parentheses.
Source: AMNDB.

The Distribution of Female Life Chances

Table 8.23 Percentage of premature births broken down by mother's height in three periods

Period	Maturity	Mother's height				
		Short	Below average	Above average	Tall	Total
1956–60	Prem.	14.8 (5 161)	12.9 (5 702)	11.5 (4 486)	11.7 (1 276)	13.0 (16 625)
1966–70	Prem.	14.4 (3 329)	12.5 (5 272)	11.6 (3 854)	10.3 (1 131)	12.5 (13 586)
1976–80	Prem.	7.3 (1 946)	6.9 (3 295)	6.1 (2 461)	5.9 (948)	6.6 (8 650)

$\chi^2 = 24.8, 19.2, 3.7$; Summary Gamma = 0.094.
Note: Sample size in parentheses.
Source: AMNDB.

8.9 HISTORICAL DATA ON LIFESTYLE

The only data available here were on smoking habits. The clear relationship evidenced between husband's social class and smoking habits in the recent period is not evident in the previous two periods (see Table 8.24). Despite

Table 8.24 Percentage of women who smoke according to husband's social class in three periods

Period	Smoking status	Husband's social class					
		Unassigned	I + II	IIIN	IIIM	IV + V	Total
1956–60	Smokes	28.6	22.5	20.1	18.9	20.8	20.2
	N	239	2 171	2 242	7 342	4 715	16 709
1966–70	Smokes	80.1	62.4	62.9	65.4	67.5	65.2
	N	297	2 207	1 298	5 357	4 495	13 654
1976–80	Smokes	48.5	28.6	33.9	47.8	61.2	47.8
	N	367	1 795	605	2 851	3 177	8 795

$\chi^2 = 23.9, 49.3, 540.6$; Summary Gamma = –0.190.
Note: Smoking data was collected differently in the period 1967–75 which may account for the larger shift observed, although it should not affect the distributions.
Source: AMNDB.

a large shift in the overall prevalence of smoking from 20 percent in the 1950s to 66 percent in the 1960s, there was no observable pattern except that the unassigned were much more likely to be smokers. In the recent period, when there is a 'clear' down gradient, the now larger unassigned group sit uncomfortably in the middle. This bodes ill for the future. The non-pattern in the earlier low-smoking period is repeated for the breakdown with height. Equally, a pattern begins to emerge, although less strongly, in the recent period (see Table 8.25).

8.10 HISTORICAL DATA ON RELATING

The pattern of *pre-nuptial* conception observed in the recent period whereby social class IIIM had the highest rate is repeated in both previous periods. The trend among the group of women unassigned to a social class grouping is erratic: whilst close to that of class IIIM in both later periods, it is the lowest in the first period (see Tables 8.26 and 8.27).

In contrast, the weak but consistent relation between mother's height and pre-nuptial conception in the recent period is repeated in the earlier periods.

8.11 HISTORICAL DATA ON PROGNOSIS

There are only birthweight data available to us in this section. In constrast to the dramatic changes in the rates of prematurity over the last three

Table 8.25 Percentage of women who smoke broken down by mother's height in three periods

Period	Smoking status	Mother's height				Total
		Short	Below average	Above average	Tall	
1956–60	Smokes	20.9	20.0	19.7	19.8	20.2
	N	5 161	5 702	4 486	1 276	16 625
1966–70	Smokes	62.2	67.1	67.8	64.8	65.9
	N	3 329	5 272	3 854	1 131	13 586
1976–80	Smokes	50.3	47.9	46.5	45.7	47.8
	N	1 946	3 295	2 461	948	8 650

χ^2 = 2.4, 30.3, 8.3; Summary Gamma = 0.034.
Source: AMNDB.

periods, the rates of low birthweight have not changed over the last two decades. However, there has been a substantial change in the proportions of low birthweight among the group of mothers unassigned to any social class.

The strong association between husbands's social class and the percentage of low birthweight in the recent period is reflected in the previous two periods with hardly any shift in the rates of low birthweight for each social class. One could assign the unassigned group to a position beyond social classes IV and V in the first and last periods, but not in the middle period. The relationship between mothers' height and low birthweight observed in the recent period was repeated in data from the earlier periods (see Tables 8.28 and 8.29).

Table 8.26 Percentage of pre-nuptial conceptions according to husband's social class in three periods

Period	Time of conception	Husband's social class					
		Unassigned	I + II	IIIN	IIIM	IV + V	Total
1956–60	PNC	3.3	3.6	6.5	9.5	8.4	7.9
	N	239	2 171	2 242	7 342	4 715	16 709
1966–70	PNC	14.1	10.0	10.9	14.5	13.8	13.2
	N	297	2 207	1 298	5 357	4 495	13 654
1976–80	PNC	11.4	4.9	6.1	11.5	9.9	9.2
	N	367	1 795	605	2 851	3 177	8 795

χ^2 = 95.7, 35.8, 68.3; Summary Gamma = 0.117.
Source: AMNDB.

Table 8.27 Percentage of pre-nuptial conceptions according to mother's height in three periods

Period	Time of conception	Mother's height				
		Short	Below average	Above average	Tall	Total
1956–60	PNC	8.8	7.7	7.4	7.1	7.9
	N	5 161	5 702	4 486	1 276	16 625
1966–70	PNC	14.1	13.2	12.7	12.3	13.2
	N	3 329	5 272	3 854	1 131	13 586
1976–80	PNC	10.3	9.8	8.7	6.9	9.3
	N	1 946	3 295	2 461	948	8 650

χ^2 = 11.1; Summary Gamma = –0.049.
Source: AMNDB.

Table 8.28 Percentage of low birthweight according to husband's social class in three periods

Period	Birthweight	Unassigned	I + II	IIIN	IIIM	IV + V	Total
1956–60	Low	13.4	5.0	5.7	6.2	9.2	6.9
	N	239	2 167	2 239	7 332	4 707	16 684
1966–70	Low	7.5	5.8	5.2	7.7	9.9	7.9
	N	295	2 206	1 298	5 356	4 494	13 649
1976–80	Low	9.0	4.7	5.5	6.9	9.3	7.3
	N	367	1 794	605	2 851	3 177	8 794

$\chi^2 = 77.2, 51.3, 42.4$; Summary Gamma = 0.166.
Source: AMNDB.

Table 8.29 Percentage of low birthweight according to mother's height in three periods

Period	Birthweight	Short	Below average	Above average	Tall	Total
1956–60	Low	9.2	6.5	5.4	4.0	6.9
	N	5 152	5 693	4 482	1 273	16 600
1966–70	Low	10.7	7.8	6.1	4.7	7.8
	N	3 327	5 271	3 853	1 131	13 582
1976–80	Low	10.1	7.7	5.6	4.4	7.3
	N	1 946	3 294	2 461	948	8 649

$\chi^2 = 75.1, 71.1, 45.1$; Summary Gamma = –0.205.
Source: AMNDB.

8.12 CONCLUSION

The purpose of this chapter was to assess the extent to which the woman's height provides an efficient discriminator of outcomes as compared to husband's social class. It was argued in Chapter 7 that an index of social class would usually be expected to discriminate most socially valued outcomes and, accordingly, a wide range of data have been presented as a 'test' of the empirical properties of HORG.

There are no clear criteria for assessing the comparative performance of indices across such a wide range of outcomes. Clearly, we *could* carry out a multivariate analysis of variance with many dependent variables and husband's social class and woman's height as the two independent variables, but this would involve extensive assumptions about the comparative weights to be attached to the different outcome measures and about the commensurability of their metrics. Instead, we have taken a more qualitative view of the task of making a comparative assessment.

On the whole, if we ignore the unassigned class – those women who have lost or otherwise mislaid their husband's classificatory tag – HORG performs well. It usually discriminates the top from the bottom – in the right direction – and, whilst there are reversals between the manual and non-manual groups within class III, they are not often substantial. Moreover, more detailed analyses show that within sub-groups defined either by schooling or by the woman's own height, husband's social class nearly always retains a gradient.

However, the initial caveat about HORG is very important: it must be remembered that the usual assignment of a HORG 'class' to women combines a variety a of classification systems. Where assignment is more correctly made on only one basis, there is always a residual group. For those data where there are 'unassigned' groups – usually the married – who could be clearly distinguished, we have shown that:

1. the unassigned group is sometimes worse off than any other group and is sometimes in the middle in no systematic fashion;
2. within the unassigned group, maternal height discriminates outcomes, and not only pregnancy-related outcomes.

The gradients with the woman's height are weaker. Within social class groups (as defined by HORG), women's height clearly discriminates in the pregancy-related outcomes (as would be expected) and retains a gradient in some, but not all, of the other characteristics. But, whilst not as effective a discriminator, women's height is both more consistent and exhaustive. There are quiet but cardinal virtues.

The 'unassigned' group are a consistent embarrassment to the HORG/SCS. Moreover, given current demographic and social trends, they are an embarrassment which is likely to increase. Even among this population of pregnant mothers – who are most likely to have a classificatory clothes-peg

98   *Constructing a Social Classification for Women*

– they have increased from 1.4 to 4.2 percent of this population between the 1950s and the 1970s.

The chapter set out from the premise that, where there is no clear underlying theoretical construct as with HORG, the empirical exploration of the power of a proposed classifier/discriminator is crucial. Yet this too can turn sour if it is taken as empirical validation of the presumed underlying but unobserved construct. This is the subject of the next chapter.

Part III
What Role does Height Play?

PROLOGUE

The previous section has given HORG all possible rope with which to hang itself, and it has duly performed. Where does this leave the theoretical arguments in support of HORG which were discussed in Chapters 2, 3, 4 and 5? That is, what does this approach have to say about the sexism of measuring women via their males (Goldthorpe's justification for HORG or a version of HORG) and about those naughty cross-class marriages?

9 A Tall Story

Our demonstration that, in purely empirical terms, the woman's own height is a consistent – although relatively weak – discriminator could be taken as a recommendation that the erstwhile investigator should sally forth with her tape measure. The implications of that possible advice are considered in more detail in the concluding chapter. Here, standing back from ourselves, we are concerned with the rather bizarre interest evidenced in the previous two chapters with characteristics of the women themselves.

In the 'real' world of social science, theorists recognise and embrace male domination. Accordingly, real theorists concerned to understand the social position of women argue that, because the man's position is much more important, a woman should be assessed in terms of her dominant male (unless she has been careless or 'unlucky').

Attempting to emulate our more learned colleagues, we therefore realise that we should not be concerned with the women's own characteristics. Instead, we should be using characteristics of the (male) head of household as a convenient index to classify the wives via their household membership (as does the HORG 'methodology', of course).

In this earnest spirit, therefore, we have examined several of the outcome measures for women used in the previous chapters relative to husbands' height. We have relied almost entirely upon the national data set of Knight (1984) as our (Aberdeen) data on husbands' height is very limited.

Here the problem of missing data is reversed, as OPCS found it was not always possible to interview both spouses. But, of course, following the standard procedure, where the woman cannot be successfully classified by the height (occupation) of the dominant male, we have used her own height (occupation). Whilst slavish emulation of the HORG procedure would imply classifying women as short or tall according to the distribution of male height (of the male labour market), we have adopted the more liberal view that women's opportunities in the height field are restricted by (physiological) forces beyond their control and have therefore classified them as short or tall by reference to their own height distribution. This measure is called HORG height.

For completeness, we have also compared the breakdowns according to his measure (HORG height) with those according to the woman's own height and an index of 'pure' husband's height. The latter index, of course, leaves many unassigned.

What Role does Height Play?

Tables 9.1 and 9.2 compare the rates for long standing illness and restricted activity in the last 14 days. None of the measures of height of husband discriminates on the restricted activity measure. But the percentage reporting long standing illness varies from 24–25 percent among the

Table 9.1 Reported disability (the GHS question) according to height

	Own height		Husband's height		HORG height	
Tall	19.3	(1 363)'	17.4	(665)	18.5	(1 322)
Above average	20.8	(1 247)	19.9	(724)	20.1	(1 321)
Below average	19.7	(1 283)	19.2	(709)	19.9	(1 299)
Short	24.6	(1 307)	26.4	(557)	25.2	(1 159)
Unassigned	–		21.2	(2 448)	–	
Total sample percentage	21.1	(5 200)	20.8	(5 103)	20.8	(5 101)
Missing values Observations with missing data				97		99

Note: Sample size in parentheses.

Table 9.2 Percentage restricted activity by various height measures

	Own height		Husband's height		HORG height	
Tall	7.9	(1 363)	8.3	(655)	8.1	(1 322)
Above average	7.7	(1 248)	8.9	(721)	8.0	(1 316)
Below average	9.2	(1 287)	7.3	(710)	8.6	(1 304)
Short	8.1	(1 307)	8.4	(559)	8.1	(1 160)
Unassigned	–		8.1	(2 449)	–	
Total sample percentage	8.2	(5 201)	8.2	(5 104)	8.2	(5 102)
Missing values				97		99

A Tall Story

'bottom' group to 17–18 percent among the 'top' social group; although it is with pure husband's height that there is the largest difference between the short and the tall.

Tables 9.3 and 9.4 present similar data for alcohol and tobacco consumption. Here the picture is more cloudy: whilst pure husband's height is a marginally more efficient discriminator than the woman's own height, HORG height is even better.

Table 9.3 Drinks less than once a week (%)

	Own height	Husband's height	HORG height
Tall	51.2 (1 375)	52.8 (668)	51.2 (1 337)
Above average	55.2 (1 258)	52.1 (725)	53.9 (1 329)
Below average	55.6 (1 297)	56.3 (712)	57.0 (1 313)
Short	54.6 (1 318)	59.9 (561)	60.2 (1 170)
Unassigned	–	54.5 (2 550)	–
Total sample percentage	55.3 (5 248)	54.7 (5 216)	55.4 (5 149)
Missing values	0	32	99

Table 9.4 Smokes now (%)

	Own height	Husband's height	HORG height
Tall	38.4 (1 371)	36.0 (666)	39.0 (1 331)
Above average	40.0 (1 252)	37.5 (722)	39.0 (1 324)
Below average	39.9 (1 289)	41.5 (710)	41.9 (1 307)
Short	41.4 (1 316)	37.0 (559)	40.0 (1 168)
Unassigned	–	41.9 (2 477)	–
Total sample percentage	39.9 (5 228)	39.9 (5 134)	40.0 (5 130)
Missing values	0	94	98

Tables 9.5 and 9.6 show the proportion who report attempting to slim during the last year and those who claim to be energetic. Slimming is obviously more of concern to those who are taller; the difference between having a tall or short husband upon one's dietary habits is startling. Yet the prize has to go to HORG height for producing the perfect gradient with no unassigneds. In contrast, the only height group who seem to make an extra effort to be energetic are those who are *aspiring* to stand tall (or above average height but not the tallest).

Table 9.5 Percentage reporting slimming during last year

	Own height	Husband's height	HORG height
Tall	31.7 (1 370)	37.3 (664)	35.9 (1 330)
Above average	30.3 (1 249)	28.3 (721)	30.1 (1 322)
Below average	31.4 (1 290)	29.5 (711)	29.5 (1 307)
Short	25.7 (1 313)	26.0 (558)	25.0 (1 165)
Unassigned	–	29.4 (2 472)	–
Total sample percentage	29.8 (5 222)	30.0 (5 126)	30.0 (5 124)
Missing values		96	98

Table 9.6 Percentage energetic by various height measures

	Own height	Husband's height	HORG height
Tall	22.8 (1 375)	20.4 (668)	22.3 (1 337)
Above average	23.4 (1 258)	24.4 (725)	24.5 (1 329)
Below average	22.5 (1 297)	20.6 (712)	22.0 (1 313)
Short	21.2 (1 318)	20.3 (561)	19.7 (1 170)
Unassigned	–	22.3 (2 550)	–
Total sample percentage	22.5 (5 248)	21.9 (5 216)	22.2 (5 149)
Missing values		32	99

Finally, Table 9.7 shows the breakdown of the proportion who are owner-occupiers by height groups. There is little to choose between the very strong gradients evidenced by all those indices.

The 'joke' works. HORG height does discriminate 'socially valued outcomes' for women; indeed, it sometimes 'works' better than husband's (and/or women's own) height. This empirical demonstration 'proves' that we should measure the husbands' height if we want to know the social position of women.

We recall that the original assumption in the classification of women in the social class scheme was that husbands and wives shared the same lifestyle (Leete and Fox, 1977). More recent theory has it that women's lifestyle is, on the whole, determined by the relationship of the household to the labour market which is (usually) best measured by the occupation of the husband as the household member most committed to the labour market. For example, Goldthorpe (1983) essentially argued on 'theoretical' grounds that women's 'class' was determined by their husbands' 'class' and then pointed to the ample evidence showing that variation in women's fortunes were determined more by their husbands' occupationally-based social class classifications. The women's occupation could therefore be ignored.

However, whilst superficially plausible, the 'logic' is very suspect. Suppose we posit that height (instead of occupation) is a good index of something 'out there' which we think is an important feature of our social structure, again on 'theoretical' grounds. A parallel 'logic' might lead us to point out that the husband's height is a good proxy measure of the household's social

Table 9.7 Whether or not owner-occupier (%)

	Own height	Husband's height	HORG height
Tall	65.6 (1 375)	74.4 (668)	64.9 (1 337)
Above average	60.3 (1 258)	68.5 (725)	61.8 (1 329)
Below average	57.2 (1 297)	62.4 (712)	56.7 (1 313)
Short	50.0 (1 318)	55.8 (561)	48.9 (1 170)
Unassigned	–	49.2 (2 550)	–
Total sample percentage	58.3 (5 248)	57.6 (5 216)	58.4 (5 149)
Missing values		32	99

location 'out there' because the husband is more closely related to structural phenomena than the woman; moreover men, being taller than women, are clearly the 'dominant' members of the household. Therefore one should use the husband's height as a reasonable proxy measure of the woman's social location 'out there'.

Furthermore, the empirical data shows us that variations in a woman's standard of living can be associated with her husband's height. Popular culture also promotes a standard view of compatibility and the rare data available on women's as well as husbands' height shows a strong association between the heights of spouses (Table 9.8). We are therefore 'entitled' to conclude that a woman's social location 'out there' can validly be indicated by her husband's height, which itself is an accurate reflection of the husband's – and household's – social location 'out there'.

This conclusion is patently absurd: empirical 'evidence' is, *pace* Goldthrope (1983), clearly slippery stuff.

Table 9.8 Height compatibility among spouses (actual and expected numbers of spouses given height distributions of men and women)

Woman's height	Husband's height					Total sample average (%)
	Tall	Above average	Below average	Short	Unknown	
Tall	253 (175.3)	212 (190.3)	134 (187.2)	85 (147.5)	669 (852.7)	1 353 (26.3)
Above average	169 (160.3)	192 (174.0)	152 (171.1)	120 (134.8)	604 (596.7)	1 237 (24.0)
Below average	146 (165.1)	175 (179.2)	207 (176.2)	145 (138.9)	601 (614.6)	1 274 (24.8)
Short	99 (166.3)	145 (180.5)	219 (177.5)	211 (139.8)	609 (618.9)	1 283 (24.9)
Total sample average	667	724	712	561	2483	5 147
(%)	(13.0)	(14.1)	(13.8)	(10.9)	(48.2)	

$\chi^2 = 173.5$, dof = 12, $p < 0.0$.
Source: Knight (1984); authors' own calculations.

The point is that both in this argument for husbands' height and in the usual argument for HORG – apart from the presumption that there is something 'out there' to be measured – a crucial phlogiston is introduced. In the case of height this was 'compatability': in the case of HORG it is the intra-household homogeneity of living standards. Both arguments are only 'evidenced' in terms of the empirical variation of womens' 'standard of living' with respect to the husband-based classifier. In neither case are *mechanisms* proposed by which either husbands' height or HORG could actually influence or be reflecting factors which influence womens' standard of living, other than a vague reference to 'compatibility' or 'intra-household homogeneity'.

Without detailed examination of the mechanisms by which a classifier discriminates, all we are left with is a set of tabulations with, usually, a gradient *to be explained*. Many have tried to explain how HORG might affect women's standard of living (compare Chapter 5 above); not only are the proposed explanations unconvincing because they rely on supposed homogamy which has never been substantiated, but they will become more unconvincing as the labour market to which these poor benighted males are continuously committed melts away.

These last two chapters have focused on the 'last resort' defence of HORG: that it works, and anyway women do marry similar men. Chapter 8 showed the difficulty of using an index which was not exhaustive and whose meaning was unclear; this chapter has shown the absurdity of relying solely on empirical associations. There is no escape from devising an index with a purpose and referent in mind.

10 The Role of Height

The rationale for the analyses using height presented earlier was a methodological one. Height has most of the characteristics which are desirable in classificatory schema, and the intention was to show that the failure of the SCS to measure up to those requirements detracted from its empirical value. Of course, we were aware that height does discriminate a range of sociobiological variables and that, at least in perinatal epidemiology, it accounts for a large proportion of the variation generally attributed to social class (see Butler and Alberman, 1969). However, we were also aware that it had no pretensions to be a measure of social status; there was certainly no respectable prior theory of social structure that would suggest the use of anthropometric data (*pace* Galton, Pearson and the whole eugenicist gang).

The empirical data in the previous chapters compared the statistical power of the women's height variables with the SCS's classification in the discrimination of socially valued outcomes. In general, height is not as 'powerful' as the social class classification, but it is more consistent and always exhaustive.

In this sense, therefore, this set of findings poses a problem akin to that facing those who seek to account for the discriminatory power of the SCS. In both cases we have the observation of variation by the index without strong prior theory which offers an explanation of the association. However, if our prior methodological argument is valid, the relative purity and clarity of height as an index should enable us to suggest mechanisms for the association. The purpose of this chapter is, then, to make some of those suggestions.

10.1 HEIGHT AS AN INDICATOR OF DEVELOPMENT

There are two issues here. In what ways does height *depend* upon previous health status and in what ways does height *predict* future health?

There is extensive evidence that height is a function of childhood nutrition. Eveleth and Tanner (1976) discuss the relative contribution of environmental and genetic influences on the basis of a worldwide survey. They conclude that whilst there is an appreciable genetic component in the variation of height between individuals (and between societies), the genetic basis of differences between groups in a society is likely to be much less pronounced. Data collected on height distribution in European societies over the last two centuries shows how height is 'a sensitive indicator of changes in welfare both for national populations and for sub groups within those populations' (Floud, 1984).

We have already shown how low birthweight is related to child's height at the age of 10 (see Table 8.18 above). There is also macro evidence from Third World countries presented in Table 10.1 that lack of access to safe water and per capita GNP are related to short height for age. Whilst one cannot rely on these ecological correlations as a basis for inference, they are large.

Moreover, it is not just a question of absolute minima (a basic diet and safe water) or a historical feature of our data referring to currently middle-aged women. Table 10.2 summarises an analysis by Carr-Hill (1988) of Knight's (1984) data. There is no obvious trend for men. For women, however, when classified by HORG the gap appears to have narrowed; but when classified by father's social class, the data, if anything, suggest a widening in the most recent period. First, these data demonstrate the permanence of height differentials despite the environmental improvements which have led to the observed secular increase in height. Second, these widely different trends both reinforce our arguments abut the ineffectiveness of HORG as a discriminator, and show the extent to which adult height depends upon early social environment. These disparate pieces of evidence provide a convincing demonstration that achieved height in early adulthood is powerfully influenced by nutritional environment whilst growing. Of course, the height attained in early adulthood is also, in part, determined by genetic factors. At a group level, however, it is clear that height can be taken as a convenient index of development, environmental and formative *influences during childhood.*

10.2 HEIGHT AND ADULT HEALTH (BEHAVIOUR)

The issue of whether height is an effective predictor of subsequent adult health is rather different. The tables presented in Chapter 8 showed a clear pattern of discrimination of health and health behaviour according to a woman's height but, following the arguments of Chapter 6, this was not taken as a demonstration that variation in height affects variations in health and in health behaviour. The mechanisms by which height 'works' have to be explained.

The clue to understanding lies in the observation that inequalities in health are emergent over the (adult) life-cycle. We know, of course, that there are substantial (ratio) inequalities in death in each adult age group

Table 10.1 Child malnutrition and other developmental indicators in seven African countries around 1980

Country	Year	% children below 80% height-for-age	GNP, 1980 $US (survey year)	Kcal per capita (2-year average around survey year)	% Access to safe water (1975)	% Adult women illiterate (most recent survey)	Infant mortality (1975–80)	Child mortality rate (around 1980)
Cameroon	1978	21.8	459	2451	26	76	114	25
Kenya	1982	24.3	312	2055	17	65	91	15
Lesotho	1976	22.0	255	2152	17	32	120	20
Liberia	1976	24.7	335	2347	20	91	160	16
Malawi	1981	31.0	201	2219	9	95	156	25
Sierra Leone	1978	31.9	–	2518	–	96	215	25
Togo	1977	24.2	303	2015	16	93	115	25

Source: Haaga, Kenrick, Test and Mason (1985).

Table 10.2 Mean heights among young adults (20–24) and difference between social class I and II and IV and V since 1940

	1940	1945	1950	1955	1960	1965	1970	1975	1980
Men									
Mean	170.4	170.7	172.6	173.0	173.8	174.4	174.7	175.0	175.5
Difference (I + II) − (IV + V)	3.9	3.0	3.9	2.9	3.4	2.4	2.5	3.2	3.1
Women									
Mean	158.4	159.5	159.8	160.6	161.1	161.3	162.0	161.9	161.5
Difference by husband's social class	3.1	3.1	3.6	3.9	2.2	1.3	3.3	2.4	1.2
Father's social class	0.4	0.8	4.0	2.9	2.4	2.7	1.7	1.2	3.1

Source: Knight (1984); data transformed by author.

(Townsend and Davidson, 1982). The pattern is not uniform: for example, the differential among over-65s is smaller. But this is usually explained in terms of the lack of relevance of the occupationally-based classification to those who are retired.

More importantly, for the argument here, whilst (ratio) inequalities might be large, the numbers of deaths involved is small at younger ages: an analysis of (ratio) inequalities in *survival* would show hardly any difference between classes at younger ages. The point is that in younger age groups most people of all social classes are healthy so that inequalities are minimal; as average population health deteriorates, differences emerge. The point can be illustrated from Knight's (1984) data comparing inequalities in two of the self-reported measures with inequalities in height (see Table 10.3). Whilst there is always a significant difference between the mean height of classes I and II as against III and IV, the differences in self-reported health are largest and most significant in middle age and almost non-existent among those aged 18–25.

This trend is confirmed by the examination of data from the West of Scotland Twenty 07 study. They interviewed and obtained physical measurements on 1009 adolescents in 1987. Very few differences were observed between social classes, except for height (see Table 10.4).

Table 10.3 Difference in height and self-reported health measures between social classes in age groups

	Mean height		Percentage reporting poor health		Percentage reporting restricted activity	
	I + II	IV + V	I + II	IV + V	I + II	IV + V
18–24	163.2	160.8	6.7	8.5	4.7	5.7
	(214)	(198)	(209)	(189)	(211)	(191)
25–34	163.2	160.3	11.9	14.8	9.0	6.6
	(304)	(201)	(302)	(198)	(301)	(196)
35–44	161.9	160.1	18.8	24.3	7.9	7.7
	(305)	(169)	(303)	(169)	(304)	(169)
45–54	162.5	158.8	20.6	30.9	8.6	11.1
	(209)	(180)	(209)	(178)	(208)	(180)
55–64	160.6	157.7	33.5	37.5	10.1	12.4
	(158)	(202)	(158)	(200)	(157)	(201)

Note: Sample sizes in parentheses.
Source: Authors' own analysis from survey of adults' heights and weights.

Table 10.3A Standard errors of difference

	Mean heights	Percentage reporting poor health	Percentage reporting restricted activity
18–24	0.613	2.67	2.23
25–34	0.545	3.10	2.42
35–44	0.596	3.99	2.57
45–54	0.623	4.45	3.05
55–64	0.630	5.08	3.35

Table 10.4 West of Scotland Twenty 07 study: per cent reporting long-standing illness mean score on the general health questionnaire (GHQ) and height by social class of parents

	% Reporting long-standing illness		Mean GHQ		Mean height	
	Boys	Girls	Boys	Girls	Boys	Girls
Non-Manual	22.4	25.0	8.4	9.6	172.7	162.9
IIIM	20.2	22.3	7.8	9.3	170.6	160.5
IV and V	28.3	17.0	8.3	9.5	170.8	161.6
Total	22.9	22.2	8.2	9.5	171.6	161.7

Source: West et al. (1990), tables 2 and 4.

The Role of Height

Not only, therefore, is height a good summary index of what happened before, it is also a *first indicator* or *emergent health disadvantage*.

10.3 HEIGHT AND SOCIAL INEQUALITIES

If height is an indicator of health mediating childhood development and a first indicator of emergent health disadvantages, its association with socially valued outcomes may be explained by an appeal to the idea that health is one aspect of generalised social inequality. Unfortunately, to examine such a hypothesis we would need an index for women which would allow us to investigate it, and if we had such an index we would not be writing this book.

One of the puzzles such an investigation might resolve was posed by Illsley's (1955) paper which suggested that there was 'selective movement between the classes at marriage such that healthy well-grown women ... tend to marry into higher social classes and small women with poorer health and physique into the lower classes' (p. 1520). Of course, this is very much a HORG-based contention, but Illsley's observation of height-related mobility at marriage in terms of the SCS in the mid-1950s does replicate in more recent data. Thus Table 10.5 shows Aberdeen data for the 1950s, 1960s and 1970s (Illsley's 1955 paper was based on Aberdeen data). In both decades there is a gradient in mean height of women across the husband's social classes within father's social class.

If it were the case that health selection of the sort Illsley suggested on the basis of height data played a part in women's achievement of social positions, health inequalities would play an important and distinctive role in stratification theory. Moreover, we would be able to offer a fuller account of the patterns of association between height and socially valued outcomes. However, we are actually unable to interpret these patterns. It may be that they really reflect, albeit imperfectly, something about the processes by which women achieve social positions: for example, that taller women are perceived as more capable during recruitment interviews (cf. also Macintyre and West, 1991). It may be that they simply reflect an aspect of assortive mating that is independent of a predominant process of social assortment: for example, by reference to some culturally-defined notions of compatibility. It may be that they are merely artefacts of the heterogeneity of the groups distinguished by the SCS which imperfectly reflect husbands' and wives' 'real' social position. As usual, the analysis of women in terms of their second-hand status raises more problems that it solves.

Table 10.5 Mean height of women by husbands' and fathers' occupational classes

1951–60

Father's class	Own husband's occupational class				
	I + II	IIIN	IIIM	IV + V	Total
I + II	161.5 (672)	161.2 (223)	160.0 (464)	159.6 (212)	160.8 (1 571)
IIIN	159.8 (286)	159.9 (198)	159.0 (665)	157.9 (458)	158.9 (1 607)
IIIM	159.0 (536)	158.6 (447)	158.0 (2 291)	157.5 (2 033)	158.0 (5 307)
IV + V	158.2 (155)	157.3 (150)	157.1 (904)	157.0 (1 381)	157.1 (2 590)
All Average (Total)	160.1 (1 649)	159.2 (1 018)	158.2 (4 324)	157.5 (4 084)	158.3 (11 075)

1961–70

Father's class	Own husband's occupational class				
	I + II	IIIN	IIIM	IV + V	Total
I + II	161.5 (664)	161.9 (201)	160.1 (574)	160.6 (404)	160.8 (1 943)
IIIN	161.6 (241)	159.2 (145)	159.9 (498)	158.0 (401)	159.2 (1 285)
IIIM	159.5 (519)	158.8 (272)	158.2 (1 693)	157.9 (1 880)	158.3 (4 364)
IV + V	160.1 (228)	158.5 (125)	157.8 (877)	157.0 (1 366)	157.6 (2 596)
All Average (Total)	160.7 (1 652)	159.7 (743)	158.5 (3 642)	157.8 (4 051)	158.7 (10 088)

1971–80

Father's class	Own husband's occupational class				
	I + II	IIIN	IIIM	IV + V	Total
I + II	161.7 (763)	161.0 (230)	160.1 (506)	160.0 (410)	160.8 (1 909)
IIIN	161.5 (202)	160.3 (76)	159.9 (229)	159.5 (290)	160.1 (867)
IIIM	160.2 (397)	160.8 (184)	158.6 (1 193)	158.7 (1 171)	159.0 (2 945)
IV + V	160.2 (254)	157.9 (97)	158.7 (803)	158.2 (1 021)	158.6 (2 175)
All Average (Total)	161.0 (1 616)	160.3 (587)	159.0 (2 901)	158.8 (2 892)	159.4 (7 896)

10.4 HEIGHT: AN ENVIRONMENTAL OR GENETIC VARIABLE?

The evidence in the first two sections of this chapter showed how height was a useful indicator for summarising patterns of development and for suggesting the kinds of factor which might be influencing adult health status. It might, however, be argued that because height is, at least in part, genetically determined it is an inappropriate variable to portray socio-economic and environmental differences.

This is not the place to resolve the genetics versus environment debates in general. However, we need to make our position clear. First, in this context, we are unashamed egalitarian environmentalists in the sense that we believe that socially valued outcomes ought to be distributed equally with complete social mobility and that the obstacles to that Utopia are entirely socio-economic and environmental. Of course, in such a Utopia, because all variation due to socio-economic and environmental factors has been expunged, the correlation between attributes of parents and children will follow the 'perfect' Mendelian pattern: in respect of height one would expect a correlation of 0.5 with each parent and a regression to the mean. In such a society, of course, there would be little point in worrying about inequalities between women or between anyone else. It is worth remarking that, at least in terms of height, Scandinavian countries do appear to have largely reached that point (Brundtland *et al.*, 1980; Lindgren 1976): according to a study of adopted children in Denmark, where environmental influences have artificially been eliminated, parents' and children's heights do follow the Mendelian patterns (Torgenson, 1990).

In contrast, in a hierarchical and impermeable society one might well find exactly the same pattern of associations between parents and children because the social groups are defined according to ascribed attributes and there is no mixing. In this case, variations in height would be predominantly explained by the extent to which environmental factors permit the attainment of genetic potential. Correlations between the heights of parents and their adult children would thus reflect the continuing inequality and impermeability of the society. Here, as we saw in the case of the eugenicists at the beginning of the century (Chapter 2 above), the powerful would portray any evidence about the flagrant inequalities as yet another demonstration of the genetic superiority of upper social groups; they may well be successful over long periods, but not for ever.

The situation in most developed countries, and particularly in the United Kingdom, is rather more messy. Whilst our societies are not hierarchical and impermeable, they are not Utopias: the (contingent?) consequence is that genetic and environmental factors are inextricably entwined in human development, and usual statistical procedures are powerless to disentangle them.

First, the point illustrated by the two extreme examples is that it is impossible to interpret a correlation between the heights of parents and children on its own. A large or an increasing correlation could indicate the non-existence/reduction of environmental disadvantage and its intergenerational transmission, or it could indicate its maintenance/increase. Without other knowledge about social trends, we are lost. Some of our readers will no doubt discern a similarity with the inconclusive arguments and controversies over the transmitted deprivation hypothesis. Second, on a practical level, we simply do not know the extent to which the variable 'parents' height' is reflecting prior social and environmental (dis)advantage, because we do not have sufficient data to tease out all the multiple ways in which (shared) environment can affect (transmitted) growth. Third, on a theoretical level, there is every reason to suppose that parent–child pairs whose genetic endowments and environmental assets do *not* 'correspond' are different from those pairs where they do.

Whilst, therefore, an individual's height is, in part, determined by the height of his or her parents, there are also strong environmental influences which co-vary with the height (social group) of the parents; and the same is true of many other individual attributes.

At first sight the difficulty of 'partialling out' the genetic effect from a height index would seem to be a good argument against using height at all. It should, however, be emphasised that, where there are mixed genetic and environmental effects, this balance has to be empirically estimated; moreover, where any other index might be referring to attributes which recur across generations – such as social class itself – the same 'partialling out' should be performed if there is no *a priori* theory of the relative effects.

Finally, it should be emphasised that, whilst it was not our purpose in this book to proffer height as a serious alternative indicator for social status, height can clearly play a useful role as both a summary and predictive indicator.

11 Implications

This monograph started out with the empirical problems of classifying women in a way that would be useful in investigations where the focus of concern was inequalities between women. We were concerned to go beyond the standard critique of the practice of using husband's occupational class to explore what would be involved in deriving a useful indicator, and to assess how the social class classification matches up to desiderata for a classification which can both display inequalities and point towards their explanations. Although the data which initially prompted this exploration were related to birth events, because our objectives were to address the methodological problems of analysing social inequalities between women in general, we have also analysed a wide range of other data. The purpose of this final chapter is to summarise what we have learnt.

It should be recalled that the concept of social class has been fundamental to any sociological description of British society for several decades now. Much of the writing focused on the class structure and its likely impact upon those at the bottom of the heap. We have largely ignored that literature, not because we think it is unimpotant but because we saw our task differently. Increasingly, debaters and polemicists have felt is necessary to instance the inequalities they are discussing with some empirical data. Since we want to be able to describe the quality of life, or socio-economic conditions in terms of the class structure, we must establish which indicator or index of class will best reflect a person's position within that 'class structure'.

It should be emphasised that this is not just an intellectual academic issue whereby researchers can better describe their data to themselves. It is a policy-relevant issue; we cannot debate policies for tackling inequalities if we cannot measure them satisfactorily (compare the introduction by Jenkin to the Black Report, 1980). And whilst most of the British data available do suggest that the social structure is not only maintaining but reproducing current inequalities in health (see Carr-Hill, 1988), differences are not immutable (see Chapter 10 above). It is important for policy to design a measure that reflects a person's position in the 'class structure' which can be used in empirical research.

11.1 THE REGISTRAR-GENERAL'S CLASS SCHEME

It is widely recognised that the Registrar-General's SCS is a rather Heath-Robinson affair, having been added to, modified and transformed through half-a-dozen Censuses. It is perhaps not so widely understood that, because it was originally designed in rather specific circumstances to address a particular set of then current issues, it was never likely to be directly appropriate for the variety of uses to which it is put three-quarters of a century later.

We have shown how Stevenson designed his classification with an eye to the set of hypotheses about fertility and infant mortality that were current in the eugenicist debate. The need for a tool apt for these purposes informed his decisions at each stage of the formulation of the scheme: hence the importance, for him, of classifying according to culture as well as by wealth, of separating out the specifically occupational content of the classification from the general influence of 'class', and of designing a single monotonic scale. Whilst these concerns are of interest, they re not necessarily the most important for deriving a classification system, and neither are they timeless.

We have seen that Stevenson's position in the early years of this century was akin to our own: he was faced with the problem of how to deploy data in such a way as to address contemporary issues whereas we are concerned with the analysis of current social inequalities between women. Indeed, in several respects, we have attempted to follow his approach. The conceptual and technical problems which he faced and resolved with a combination of intuition, perseverance and hard work provide an object-lesson in exploiting data to confront problems.

The legacy that Stevenson left, however, was not the one of a historical debate resolved or of useful methodological lessons. We have followed Stevenson through the late 1920s when he seems to have come to believe that the SCS provided an account of social reality and when the foundations of its subsequent reification and generalisation were laid.

Women were not originally included in the SCS. Seen in one light, the procedure of classifying them according to their husband's occupation can be regarded as a continuation of the intuitive, heuristic spirit that was a hallmark of the origins of the scheme of classifying men: it entailed the speculative deployment of data to address a particular issue relating to the 'purity' of the male classification. However, that project in itself depends on the reification of the male classification and contained within it the dual intention of examining the 'indirect effect of occupation on (male) mortality' and of investigating 'social class' variations in female mortality. The indicator and what it was intended to indicate were confused at the outset.

The movement from the explicit investigation of *wives* to the wholesale inclusion of women in the SCS was the product of a search for an exhaustive classification for women. The result is a mess. Depending on their circumstances, women are sometimes classified by their own (sometimes previous) occupation, sometimes by their husbands' occupations and sometimes not at all. Moreover, the priority accorded to the occupation of the male head of household is neither theoretically based nor is it supported in detail by current empirical evidence about the lives of women.

We are interested in the problems of deriving a classification of women which will point to the effects upon them of the social structure in which they live. From that perspective, it is simply silly to measure a characteristic of the husband.

Of course, in some cultures and/or in some epochs, women's lives may be totally determined by that of her husband so that it would, contingently, be appropriate to use a characteristic of the husband as an index of her own position. But to establish that, one would have to first investigate the relation between a women's social position and that of her husband, using *independent* index of the woman's social position. The problem, therefore, remains of finding an index which can provide a measure of her and which is operational.

11.2 JUSTIFICATIONS OF THE USE OF THE SOCIAL CLASS SCHEME FOR WOMEN

A major strand of the argument of this book has been to address the ways in which the use of the Registrar-General's SCS for the classification of women might be justified. We have discussed three of these in some detail.

First, it may be that SCS/HORG is a genuine indicator of social position and has been since its inception. If this were the case, it would be possible to use the scheme as a basis for exploring the extent to which empirical variation in any aspect of a woman's life is associated with her social position. For this justification to succeed, the scheme would need to be based on a strong and coherent theory which provided both an account of the nature of social position and explained why that social position was accurately measured, or precisely indicated, by the Scheme. Goldthorpe's own work has been exemplary in its attempts to operationalise consistent theoretical perspectives in this way. However, his theoretical formulation provides an account of only one aspect of the social structure – class formation – and hence of the position of women. As such, its useful application to women is limited and correctly subject to the feminist critique of class-based models of stratification.

The SCS, by contrast, has never had a coherent and articulated theoretical basis. Our attempt to discern one in Stevenson's extant accounts of the foundation of the scheme allowed us to draw some rather imprecise inferences about the underlying model of society to which it referred, a model to which few contemporary social scientists would adhere. Because of the problems our review of accounts of the inception of the SCS identified, we found Szreter's (1984) account of the early years both useful and convincing. However, the heuristic deployment of available data to address contemporary issues which Szreter describes is not the same as the operationalisation of coherent theory. We have argued that, for Stevenson, the data dictated which aspects of the issues could be addressed: the operationalisation of coherent theory requires that the theory dictates both the data and its form.

Since the SCS did not grow out of a theoretical account of the characteristics it was supposed to measure or indicate, the justification of its use that it is a genuine indicator of 'social position' is untestable and unexaminable, and will therefore simply not stand up. It is, however, possible that, for men at least, Stevenson may have stumbled across a genuine indicator of 'social position'. If we follow Szreter's argument, it was the case that Stevenson himself came to believe that. The justification for Stevenson was the empirical one that it discriminated aspects of reproductive behaviour and mortality: the contemporary form of this argument is discussed below as the third possible justification of the use of the Scheme.

Putting the empirical argument to one side for the moment, even if it were the case that the Scheme happened to provide a good indicator for men, its application to women would required justification. This second justification rests on two interlinked propositions, the first being that the overwhelming majority of marriages are class homogenous, and the second that the social position of women is entirely dependent on the social position of the (male) head of the household in which they live.

The first of these propositions is relatively easy to test so long as the second proposition holds good. The test consists of the comparison of a woman's father's class with that of her husband. In common with every examination of this cross-tabulation we have shown that, simplistically, there is insufficient class homogamy on this basis to sustain the justification. Of course, that formulation denies women the possibility of intergenerational mobility in their own right pre-maritally. Unfortunately, the only indicator of this within the SCS is the woman's own occupational class; but, because of labour market segmentation and because of the relationship between mobility and age, the use of the classification for women's occupations has been subjected to devastating criticism. Goldthorpe may be right in saying that interclass marriages are artefacts of inappropriate classification but, in the absence of a theoretical statement of what the SCS is supposed to measure, there is no way of examining this contention.

The absence of a theoretical position also means that there are no criteria for examining the second proposition: that women share the social position of their husbands. However, those studies (such as Pahl, 1980; and Pahl 1983) which have addressed issues of household homogeneity in terms of factors which one would expect to be associated with social position (consumption or political attitudes and behaviour, for example) have found extensive heterogeneity within households. Some have argued that social positions have different correlates for men and women in contemporary society (see Abbott and Sapsford, 1987, for a review); but this begs the question of what is meant by social position.

The final justification for the use of the SCS is that it works. HORG *does* discriminate across a wide range of socially valued outcomes and characteristics. As HORG works, the *purely empirical* justification should have desirable methodological consequences: that is, it ought to be possible to use the discriminatory power of HORG to investigate those characteristics which are associated with the unequal distribution of the benefits of society.

Our critique of the empirical power of HORG has shown how it 'works' patchily and unevenly, which makes it impossible to specify its range or power in a way that would contribute to theory. In particular, although one of the defences of the SCS is that it provides 'continuity' over time, the distribution of several of the 'outcome' variables considered have not behaved in the same way over the last 30 years. The empirical properties of the classification violates its apparent methodological usefulness (see further discussion in sections 11.4 and 11.6 below). The comparison with height, which has the technical properties which are desirable in a classificatory scheme, has shown in detail the the empirical consequences of not meeting those desiderata. In the end the answer to this final justification, that the scheme 'works' when applied to women, is 'so what?'

11.3 OTHER POSSIBLE SCHEMA

Of course, the idea that there are problems with the SCS as it is applied to women is far from novel. The observation has spawned a plethora of theoretical writing and several attempts to derive indices which are more appropriate to women, some of which are discussed below. We are only too aware of the inherent problems of the area and of the constraints imposed by data.

It is, nevertheless, clear that the problems faced by those who start from the proposition that what is sought is a method of locating women in the occupational system are legion, whether that is thought of in terms of their relations to the means of production or of hierarchies of occupational prestige. Although the position of single women appears relatively straightforward, the position of all women in the labour market is affected by the fact of labour market segmentation: some women do marry and it is a characteristic of contemporary society that women are subjected not only to the exigencies of reproduction but also to the nursing of both child and husband: women as a whole are restricted in their career opportunities. The predominance of life-cycle stage as an explanatory factor in patterns of women's employment (see, for example, Martin and Roberts, 1984) means that the significance of women's occupations as an indicator of anything (except perhaps her age) is far from clear. This inherent lack of clarity makes women's occupations treacherous components of an indicator.

One way of coping with some of the difficulties has been suggested by Roberts (1986, 1987), who seeks to classify women according to the work they do. 'The work they do' is not restricted to paid employment, but takes account of 'household work'. In particular the scheme uses, as an indicator, the fact that women's unpaid work changes with the age of any children in the household.

This classification has the advantage of being firmly based in the work women do, although it is acknowledged that the indicator used is far from perfect. Moreover, in detail, the scheme does take account of the important distinction between full- and part-time work. In terms of the argument of this book, however, it does suffer from several disadvantages. For example, both employment and the measure of domestic responsibilities are closely related to life-cycle stage and the scheme inevitably confounds life-cycle and 'class'. As Roberts herself points out, the indicator for household work means that the scheme is inappropriate for the analysis of reproduction behaviour. Importantly, it continues to mask inequalities between full-time housewives: by far the majority of these women (99 percent in the 1986 version) fall into one class (class 3).

There is, however, a more fundamental difficulty with this approach. We believe that it confuses the properties of the indicator with what it is intended to indicate. The argument is that unpaid domestic labour is just as (and often more) arduous and productive as paid employment: it is an argument with which we would agree. However, the meaning of paid employment which justifies its use as a class indicator does not lie in the hours worked or in its contribution to the well-being of society as a whole. It is not the characteristics of paid employment *per se* that are of interest: it is rather what occupation indicates about an individual's location in the social structure. Quite apart from the difficulties of finding an indicator for unpaid domestic labour, it is far from obvious that (even if one had such a thing) it would provide a viable indicator of social position. It would certainly not share a common metric with what was indicated by paid employment on the grounds of similarities in the content and characteristics of paid and unpaid labour.

Another approach to the problem is to retain the household as the unit of class analysis. In some versions (such as Britten and Heath, 1983; Pahl and Wallace, 1985) a joint class is calculated on the basis of the employment of both partners. These approaches do not solve the problem of finding an appropriate method of classifying women's occupations. Moreover, they rely on the assumption of household homogeneity and, as noted above, both in terms of patterns of consumption (Pahl, 1980; and Pahl 1983) and 'social imagery' (Porter, 1983), it is increasingly difficult to sustain.

The latter criticism also applies to the 'dominance' principle suggested by Erikson (1984) and used by Goldthorpe and Payne (1986). In this version the class of a household is not automatically determined by its male head but by the occupation of the person with the 'highest' social class within the household (with the proviso that this person should work full-time and be 'committed to the labour market'). Since this involves only marginal recoding of the minority of cases where women fulfil the stringent conditions of 'dominance', in practice the scheme looks very like the 'conventional view' and is subject to the same critique.

The fact that current methods of occupational classification do not take account of 'women's' occupations adequately has provided the starting point for several attempts to produce more refined building blocks for occupationally-based classifications. The effects of labour market segmentation have been explored by Murgatroyd (1982) in relation to the concept of 'skill', a concept whose inherent gender bias was suggested by Phillips and Taylor (1980). Even so fundamental a division as the manual/non-manual divide has been questioned in relation to women's employment. As Arber, Dale and Gilbert (1986) point out, a division that ranks supermarket check-out operatives (the Registrar-General's social class IIIN) 'above' air-hostesses (the Registrar-General's social class IV) is not even intuitively sensible. Some of the building blocks are simply too heterogeneous for 'women's occupations': untrained nursing auxiliaries and Senior Nursing Officers are classified in the same occupation group.

With these difficulties in mind, the group at Surrey University have ranked women's occupations according to wage levels, typical educational qualifications and fringe benefits to produce a scale that clearly distinguishes full- and part-time work and the differences between male and female workers (Dale, Gilbert and Arber, 1983). More recently, the group have developed a scale of occupational class which is intended to classify both men and women but which distinguishes between women's jobs more adequately than the current scale (Arber, Dale and Gilbert, 1986).

This, continuing, work provides valuable and detailed information about labour market segmentation and the classification broadly reflects equivalent labour market positions. The labour market position of an individual, however, is seen as distinct from the 'consumer class' of the household of which she is a part. Conceptually 'consumer class' is thought of as the effects of the inputs from all members of the family (wages and domestic labour) as well as the patterns of expenditure it adopts (Dale, Gilbert and Arber, 1983, p. 7). The relationship between labour market position and consumer class remains a matter for investigation. The work of the Surrey Group demonstrates the advantages of the sophisticated deployment of extensive data to pose and answer questions. However, unless the work can provide relatively simple indicators, the extensive requirement for household information precludes the use of 'consumer class', either alone or in conjunction with labour market class, for many research situations. Moreover, the relationship between expressive and conceivable measures of the quality of life means that the use of such an index may be restricted to discriminating only a sub-set of outcomes.

11.4 DESIDERATA FOR A CLASSIFICATION

Prior to devising a classification, it is important to emphasise that every classificatory scheme responds to a particular set of questions in the context of a particular view of the world. It is, at the very least, incumbent on investigators to examine the appropriateness of the measures they use to the questions that they want to address. But, in any specific situation, it is often possible to devise a scheme of classification that is uniquely appropriate to the problem in hand.

There are, of course, particular difficulties associated with the measurement and discrimination of generalised inequality between women. A measure has to be devised which will be useful across several fields. Nevertheless the point should be emphasised that the intended range of discrimination of a classification should be made explicit, otherwise failures to discriminate can easily be explained away. For example, we have argued in Chapters 6 and 7 that an index, to be useful in the context of investigating generalised inequality among women, should be capable of discriminating outcomes in the areas of health, learning, material possessions, opportunities, relationships and future prognosis for the woman's family where appropriate. We do not expect everyone to agree with our detailed argument. However, the methodological point is that it is important to attempt to describe the main aspects of 'life quality' which are relevant for women *before* searching for the appropriate general measure.

The other desiderata, considered in Chapter 6, are more technical. First, where the variable proposed as an indicator of social position is also supposed to provide an explanation of social patterning, the nature of that explanation should be unambiguous. The occupationally based social class measures tend to be used that way, for example, when researchers 'control for' social class without further explanation of how social class variation is accounting for the observed patterning. Second, an index should not allow circular explanations of the following kind: social class discriminates between the quality of life of different people because the quality of life is associated with the features that distinguish the characteristics of the social class index in the real world. Third, the basis of the classification should be uniform. The basis of any classification defines the ways in which the groups it distinguishes are alike. If the basis is not uniform, the fundamental rationale for classification is lost. Fourth, an index should provide a unique assignment for everyone. Whilst the set of rules elaborated by the OPCS does provide a unique assignment for all women (at least in principle), it is at the expense of uniformity of criteria and clarity of meaning. Fifth, movements in the value for an index should correspond to changes in the underlying phenomena it is intended to indicate. Because this proposition is difficult to test it is difficult to be over rigorous: nevertheless it is reasonable to ask that the index should be relatively sensitive to 'real' changes and relatively stable when there are not 'real changes'. Sixth, it should be easy to collect the information on which the classification is based within the context of the study being undertaken; such is manifestly not the case with the SCS. Seventh, quantitiative scales ought to reflect the conception of the underlying phenomena in their form and, where the intention is to use them in statistical analysis, they ought to be devised with an eye to the technical constraints imposed by the analysis being envisaged.

These requirements are not fulfilled by the Registrar-General's SCS, and neither is there any likelihood of modifications resolving the problems.

11.5 A TALL STORY

The Registrar-General's classification is not only theoretically flawed but empirically very difficult to interpret. The problem remains, therefore, of developing an index for female social status which can be used in a routine fashion in social surveys and which will reflect female social status.

In Chapter 6, a number of possibilities were considered. Where the problem is to devise an index of household social status, there are a number of options such as car ownership and tenure status. But the field of choice for describing an *individual's* position is much more limited. Almost any conceivable index of an *individual's* position will also form part of the construction of the *household* position so that the individual component index cannot be directly interpreted. An obvious example is income. Whilst this might be seen as the perfect individualistic characteristic, the issue is the amount of income over which the individual has control, and the relation between disposable income (in that sense) and share of equivalent household income varies widely between men and women, and between sub-cultures in, mostly, unknown ways.

One possible candidate which avoids these criticisms is education. This is clearly a property of the individual. The difficulty is that it is a very 'lumpy' measure as the bulk of the population left school at the minimum school-leaving age.

There were no obvious candidates in our data: in consequence, in our substantive work upon birthweight (see Carr-Hill and Pritchard, 1985), we focused on a model in which social class played only a peripheral role by considering it only after other birth-relevant characteristics of the mother, such as her age, height and weight. This approach produced consistent and reliable results; whilst previous attempts to focus on social class as the main influencing factor led to erratic results, essentially mother's height had a strong effect on birthweight and would supplant social class even if the latter were entered first into the model.

There are good empirical and theoretical reasons for this. It is an auxalogual (growth-related) truism to say that height is on average socially determined and reflects social and economic conditions. Earlier work on 'our' Aberdeen data had shown how height 'mediated' a process of social mobility (Illsley, 1955), and this is confirmed in more recent data. Moreover, in demonstrating the appropriateness of a classification, height satisfied nearly all the technical desiderata outlined above, with the exception of its relative sensitivity to changes in an individual's standard of living over time. In this book, therefore, we turned to examining the possibility that

Implications 127

height might act as a useful empirical index of attained status in early adulthood.

Chapter 8 compared the empirical 'performance' of mothers' height and husbands' social class in disseminating valued outcomes (see above). We showed how mothers' height was a consistent discriminator although usually weaker than HORG; in contrast, whilst it is possible to display wide differences in respect of most characteristics between the Registrar-General's social classes I and II and IV and V, those (un)fortunate women who have lost or mislaid their classificatory clothes peg, or are otherwise classified as 'unknown', do not show a consistent pattern: they are sometimes in the middle, sometimes at the bottom. According to conventional methodological criteria, therefore, height is a 'better' discriminator simply because it is more consistent. No one – the (male) authors least of all – would want to suggest that height should *supplant* social class in empirical writings, but (according to the conventional methodological criteria) height ought to be taken seriously as an 'index' for discriminating valued outcomes. This empirical performance of such an unlikely characteristic should make investigators wary of deploying social class data in this kind of exercise.

Finally, to emphasise the poverty of that view, we emulated the current logic for retaining HORG as a valuable index for women, using husband's height as the classifier. Chapter 9 shows how the same line of argument as described in Chapter 4 and 5 for HORG would lead us to the conclusion that men's height determines women's height. Whilst this might satisfy some of the more reptilian instincts among a fraction of our readers, we take that as a convincing demonstration of the need to think about what you are doing before you classify.

In particular, whilst we would not want to advance height as a universal panacea to the problem of classification, we should be clear that, in searching for a measure of 'social classness', we should be looking for some index that has many of the characteristics of height: that is, it should be hierarchical, exhaustive, non-circular, and so on.

11.6 IMPLICATIONS FOR THEORY AND EMPIRICAL RESEARCH

We think that we have demonstrated the silliness of measuring men (husbands) when the purpose of an analysis is to talk about women. Moreover, we think that the erratic behaviour of the 'unclassified' group points to a problem with an occupationally-based classification which will grow as full-time employment continues to decrease. The Registrar-General's SCS will no longer be adequate to describe the standard of living for men, let alone for their spouses. What implications does this have for theory and for empirical research?

11.6.1 Theory

Clearly, the empirical investigation of one peculiar aspect of the social class classification cannot solve large theoretical problems, but we think we have illuminated some issues. First, when a classification is used in a large variety of empirical settings, it is prone to being reified. It cannot be repeated too often that, at best, a classification should be designed to answer a question. Where the possibility of comparison with other studies is seen as very important, so that an off-the-shelf classification or index like the SCS is used, then it is always an empirical question whether or not the classification discriminates. Conceptually, problems of comparison over time or between populations are not simply solved by using the same indicator of 'social class'. Furthermore, as noted below (p. 178), the technical problem of using complex coding schemes with data that may not be collected uniformly will also tend to undermine the value of comparisons.

Second, the mechanism by which a classification discriminates outcomes always needs to be explained and cannot be presumed from the nature of the classification. This is particularly confusing with an occupationally-based social class measure which nowadays provides a snapshot of a rapidly changing world. Whilst, sometimes, we only want a classification to tell us where we are at now, today, more frequently we expect our index to tell us something about a cluster of characteristics (something akin to Stevenson's culture and wealth which will have accumulated over a longish period).

These two criticisms are, of course, especially pertinent when using an index such as height. There are an obvious series of temptations to imbue height with a social meaning all of its own. A frivolous example of this is the perceived necessity for Prince Charles to stand one step higher than Diana for their photographs; more seriously our analysis of the data in Chapter 10 suggests that height might be playing a social role quite independent of any physiological meaning.

In addition, there is the issue of explaining the mechanisms or processes by which height might be associated with health-related variables. There is a wealth of historical evidence linking overall levels of socio-economic development and height (for example Floud, 1984; Eveleth and Tanner, 1976): Carr-Hill, Fraser and Russell (1984) have shown how low birthweight affects height at the age 10 even after allowing for many other intervening variables; and several macro studies in the Third World have shown the link between stunting (low height for age) and access to safe water and nutritional levels. Whilst there are difficulties in sorting out the relative contribution of genetics and environment to individual growth (see section 10.4 above), the fact that growth depends upon a range of developmental, environmental and socio-economic variables is not in doubt. The question is how do variations in attained height act upon subsequent (mid-life) health?

Once again, there are frivolous explanations of the bar-propping variety (pubs and their counter levels were built when people were shorter and so are more accessible to the short, which is why they drink more), but it is hard to find any more coherent accounts of the link between height when a young adult and subsequent health status. The appropriate conclusion is that height is acting as a summary index for all the formative influences upon development which themselves are likely to have an impact upon later health. Thus, poor housing in childhood may itself be prognostic of morbidity when an adult; similarly, bad eating habits when young have a tendency to recur when older. Whilst there are several competing explanations for these associations, in the absence of extensive longitudinal data it may be appropriate to use height as a reasonable proxy for these developmental and environmental formative influences.

11.6.3 Empirical Research

One lesson is very simple. Go forth and mensurate. Height – and other physiological characteristics – can be measured reliably and simply on large populations. They provide useful 'objective' health information, so it is silly to omit them.

There is, of course, a growing awareness of the importance of using physiological measures in debates about inequalities in health. For example, Macintyre (1988) analyses the socio-economic correlates with physiological characteristics (blood pressure, height and lung function); and in 1984 HALS put a lot of effort into collecting baseline physiological data on a large population sample (Cox, Blaxter, Buckle et al. 1987).

The argument here goes further, of course; we are suggesting that in certain circumstances where other measures of social classification are losing their meaning, height provides a useful summary index of background, family and growth. Where no other data exist, it may be sensible to use height as an index.

The other major lesson is the importance of being very careful in the secondary (meta-)analysis of several sets of data. Whether or not the same measure is intended, the way in which the data is gathered and in which the measure has been interpreted means that comparison of results from the analysis of different sets of data is fraught with difficulties.

This is a particular problem in the case of comparisons of results where the social class index has been used. For example, when analysing occupational mortality, there is no way of knowing whether the practices of assigning social class in Aberdeen and in Aberystwyth are the same, even though the clerical staff are following the same set of instructions. In fact, the analysis by Prior (1985) of coding practices at Dublin General Registry Office would suggest that there is substantial scope for 'discretionary' coding. Furthermore, the ways in which their instructions are applied will vary over time so that intercensal comparisons – a favourite for inequality analysts – are especially prone to the dangers of interpreting artefactual changes.

The situation is no better when comparing research data sets, for the raw data requirements to construct the occupational social class measure are extensive. Where data has been collected with a different (set of) question(s), there is no guarantee that the data will be comparable; indeed, it is only recently that social researchers have adopted a standard set of questions to elicit the basic data for constructing the social class variable (Hoinville and Jowell, 1986).

There is, however, no guarantee that this 'standard' set of questions will continue to be used by its originators. As was shown in Chapter 3, the recent proposed changes to CODOT emphasise the occupational skill content of a job rather than its location in an occupational structure.

The emphasis upon the occupational skill content is peculiarly reminiscent of Stevenson's initial concern to develop both a personal and an industrial classification. Has the OPCS learnt nothing from 100 years' experience?

More seriously, classifications by 'social class' will become increasingly irrelevant to those concerned to portray and account for social inequalities. As has been emphasised at several points throughout the book, where it is important to measure 'social classness' then off-the-shelf indicators are usually inappropriate; researchers must ensure that the index they are using to demonstrate inequalities are adequate to that task. Unsurprisingly, it is unlikely that the government will provide.

11.7 DESCRIBING AND EXPLAINING INEQUALITIES

This book was undertaken in the belief that describing and explaining inequalities between women are important projects that should be addressed in empirical research. They are not only important in their own right, as accounts of society at the end of the twentieth century, but also because

Implications

inequality is pervasive and impinges upon virtually any social phenomenon which research may investigate. In the end, we believe that a sense of inequalities should inform what researchers do.

To those accustomed to the debate about the nature of social class in general and what the concept might mean when applied to women in particular, our approach may seem atheoretical and barren. We admire and respect these concerted attempts to provide conceptual rigour in sociological theory. It is, however, true to say that we are frustrated with purist Marxist, Weberian, neo-Marxist, neo-Weberian (and so on) formulations and reformulations, and with debates about the relative priority of capitalism and patriarchy in the situation of women. Our frustration stems from our belief that these academic pursuits have become divorced from our central problematic of inequality and from empirical research.

On the other hand, our examination of measures available for empirical research has become a catalogue of their inadequacies. Conceptually, theoretically, analytically and operationally we have not found any empirical scheme which meets even the minimum criteria of a useful empirical level. Off-the-peg solutions should be treated with caution and with explicit scepticism.

For those actually engaged in the business of research who feel cheated that a book with the subtitle 'The Empirical Problem of Female Social Class' does not offer another new prescription, our message is not a comfortable one. You are on your own with your problem and the value and quality of your solution depends on your acuity, creativity and craftsmanship. We hope however, that this book will contribute to the difficult choices you have to make.

References

Abbott, P. and Sapsford, R. (1987), *Women and Social Class*, London, Tavistock.
Ansell, C. (1874), *Statistics of Families in the Upper and Professional Classes*, London, Blades.
Arber, S., Dale, A. and Gilbert, G. N. (1986), 'The limitations of existing social class: classifications of women'. In A. Jacoby (ed.), *The Measurement of Social Class: Proceedings of a Conference*, Guildford, Social Research Association.
Berent, J. (1954), 'Social mobility and marriage: a study of trends in England and Wales'. In D. V. Glass (ed.) (1954), *Social Mobility in Britain*, London, Tavistock.
Blaxter, M. (1986), 'Longitudinal studies in Britain relevant to inequalities in health'. In R. Wilkinson (ed.) (1986), *Class and Health*, London, Tavistock.
Boston, G. (1980) 'Classification of occupation', *Population Trends*, 20, pp. 9–11.
Britten, N. and Heath, A. (1983), 'Women, men and social class'. In E. Garmarnikov et al. (eds), *Gender, Class and Work*, London, Heinemann, pp. 46–60.
Brundtland, C. H., Liestol, K. and Walloe, L. (1980), 'Height, weight and menarcheal age of Oslo schoolchildren during the last 60 years', *Annals of Human Biology*, 7, p. 307.
Butler, N. L. and Alberman, E. D. (1969), *Perinatal Problems*. Edinburgh, Livingstone.
Carr-Hill, R. A. (1983), *Indicators of Health and of Inequalities in Health*, presented to the SSRC Workshop on Inequalities in Health, Royal Society of Medicine, London, November.
Carr-Hill, R. A. (1987), 'The inequalities in health debate: a critical review of the issues', *Journal of Social Policy*, 16, 4, pp. 509–42.
Carr-Hill R. A. (1988), 'Time trends in inequalities in health' *Journal of Biosocial Science*, July, 20, 3, pp. 265–73.
Carr-Hill, R. A., Fraser, C. and Russell, M. (1984) 'The influence of factors associated with low birth weight on development at the age of ten years', in Illsley and Mitchell, *Low Birthweight*.
Carr-Hill, R. A. and Pritchard, C. W. (1985) *The Development and Exploitation of Empirical Birthweight Standards*, London, Macmillan.
Carr-Hill, R. A. and Lintott, J. (1987) 'Measuring health and human activities', *Proceedings of Annual Conference of the Leisure Studies Association*, University of Sheffield.
Cartwright, A. and Anderson R. (1981) *General Practice Revisited: A Second Study of Patients and their Doctors*, London, Tavistock.
Central Advisory Council for Education (1967) *Children and their Primary Schools*, Vols 1 & 2 (Chairperson: Lady B. Plowden), London, HMSO, 1967
Coleman, D. A. (1977), 'Assortive mating in Britain', in R. Chester and J. Peel, *Equalities and Inequalities in Family Life*, London, Academic Press.
Collett, C. E. (1902), *Educated Working Women: Essays on the Economic Position of Women Workers in the Middle Classes*, London, King.
Cox, B, Blaxter, M. and Buckle, E. et al. (1987) *The Health and Life Style Survey*, London Health Promotion Research Trust.
Dale, A., Gilbert, G. N. and Arber, S. (1983), *Alternative Approaches to the Meas-*

References

urement of Social Class for Women and Families, Report to the EOC, October 1983.

Delphy, C. (1977), *The Main Enemy: A Materialist Analysis of Women's Oppression*, London, Women's Research and Resources Centre Publications.

Department of Education and Science (1967) *Children and their Primary Schools* (The Plowder Report) Chaired by Lady Plowder JP.

Dex, S. (1985), *The Sexual Division of Work*, Brighton, Wheatsheaf.

DHSS (1980) *Inequalities in Health, Report of a Research Working Group* (The Black Report) Chaired by Sir Douglas Black. Foreword by Patrick Jenkin, Secretary of State for Social Services.

Dowding, V. M. (1981), 'New assessment of the effects of birth order and socioeconomic status on birth weight', *British Medical Journal*, 282, pp. 683–6.

Dunbar, W. C. (1907), 68th Annual Report of the Registrar-General.

Duncan, O. D. (1966), 'Path analysis: sociological examples', *American Journal of Sociology*, 72, pp. 1–16.

Erikson, R. (1984), 'The social class of men, women and families', *Sociology*, 18, pp. 500–14.

Eveleth, P. B. and Tanner, J. M. (1976), *Worldwide Variation in Human Growth*, Cambridge University Press.

Floud, R. (1984), *Measuring the Transformation of European Economies: Income, Health and Welfare*, Discussion Paper Series No. 33, London, Centre for Economic Policy and Research.

Fox, A. J. (1984), 'Social mobility around the time one had children' (published in Longitudinal Study No. 2) London, OPCS, HMSO.

Galton, F. (1901), 'The possible improvement of the human breed under the existing conditions of law and sentiment', *Nature*, 64, 1670, pp. 659–65.

General Registry Office, *Registrar-General's Decennial Supplements for 1901, 1911 and 1921*, London, HMSO.

Glass, D. V. (1954), *Social Mobility in Britain*, London, Routledge & Kegan Paul.

Goldblatt, P. (1988), 'Mortality and social classification', ESRC Survey Methods, Seminar Series, Report of March 1988 Seminar.

Goldthorpe, J. (1983), 'Women and class analysis in defence of the conventional view', *Sociology*, 17, pp. 465–88.

Goldthorpe, J. (1984), 'Women and class analysis: a reply to the replies', *Sociology*, 18, pp. 491–9.

Goldthrope, J. and Payne, C. (1986), 'On the class mobility of women: results from different approaches to the analysis of recent British data', *Sociology*, 20, pp. 531–55.

Greenwood, H. P. (1936), *Employment and the Depressed Areas*, London, Routledge.

Haaga, J., Kenrick, C., Test, K. and Mason, J. (1985), 'An estimate of the prevalence of child malnutrition in developing countries', *World Health Statistics Quarterly*, 38.

Hall, J. and Jones, D. C. (1950), 'Social grading of occupations', *British Journal of Sociology*, I, March 1950.

Harre, R. (1964), *Matter and Method*, London, Macmillan.

Hart, N. (1986), 'Inequalities in health: the individual and the environment', *Journal of the Royal Statistical Society* Ser. A, 14, p. 228.

Haskey, J. (1987), 'Trends in marriage and divorce in England and Wales 1837–1987', *Population Trends*, 48, Summer 1987, pp. 11–19.

References

Heath, A. (1981) *Social Mobility*, London, Fontana.
Heath, A. and Britten, N. (1984), 'Women's jobs do make a difference', *Sociology*, 18, pp. 475–90.
Hindness, B. (1973), *The Use of Official Statistics in Sociology*, London, Macmillan.
Hoem, J. M. and Rennermalm, B. (1985), 'Modern family initiation in Sweden: experience of women born between 1936 and 1960', *European Journal of Population*, 1, 81, p. 112.
Hoinville, G. and Jowell, R. (1985) *Survey Research Practice*, Aldershot, Gower.
Hope, K. and Goldthorpe, J. (1974), *The Social Grading of Occupations: A New Approach and Scale*, Oxford, Clarendon Press.
Humphreys, N. A. (1887), 'Class mortality statistics', *Journal of the Royal Statistical Society*, L, June, pp. 255–92.
Illsley, R. (1955), 'Social class and selection', *British Medical Journal*, II, pp. 15–20.
Illsley, R. (1986), 'Occupational class, selection and the production of inequalities', *Quarterly Journal of Social Affairs*, 2, pp. 27–49.
Illsley, R. and Carr-Hill, R. A. (forthcoming), *Health and Social Mobility*.
Illsley, R. and Mitchell, R. D. (1984) (eds), *Low Birthweight: A Medical and Psychological Study*, Chichester, John Wiley.
Jones, I. G. and Cameron, D. (1984), 'Social class: an embarrassment to epidemiology?', *Community Medicine*, 6, pp. 37–46.
Kendrick et al., cited in Payne, G. and Payne, J. (1981), 'Mobility, employment and the class structure', BSA Conference on Capital and Class in Scotland, Aberdeen, March 1981.
Knight, I. (1984), *The Heights and Weights of Adults in Great Britain*, London, OPCS, HMSO.
Leete, A. and Fox, J. (1977), 'Registrar General's social class: origins and uses', *Population Trends*, 18, pp. 1–7.
Lindgren, G. (1976), 'Height, weight and menarche in Swedish schoolchildren in relation to socio-economic and regional factors', *Annals of Human Biology*, 3, pp. 501–28.
McDowell, M. (1981), 'Measuring women's occupational mortality', *Population Trends*, 34.
Macfarlane, A. (1980), 'Official statistics and women's health and illness', EOC Research Bulletin, 4, pp. 43–77, Manchester.
Macfarlane, A. and Mugford, M. (1984) *Birth Counts: Statistics of Pregnancy and Birth Events*, London, HMSO.
Macintyre, S. (1988), *Social Correlates of Human Height*, Oxford, Sci. Prog.
Macintyre, S. and West, P. (1991) 'Social developmental and health correlates of "attractiveness" in adolescence', *Sociology of Health and Illness*.
Mack, J. and Lansley, S. (1985), *Poor Britain*, London, Allen & Unwin.
Martin, J. and Roberts, C. (1984), *Women and Employment: A Lifetime Perspective*, London, HMSO.
Miles, I. (1985) *Social Indicators for Human Development*, London, Pinter.
Murgatroyd, L. (1982), 'Gender and occupational stratification', *Sociological Review*, 30, pp. 574–602.
Nissel, M. (1980), 'Women in government statistics: basic concepts and assumptions', EOC Research Bulletin, 4, pp. 5–28, Manchester.
Oakley, A. (1981), *Subject Women*, Oxford, Robertson.

References

Oakley, A. and Oakley, R. (1979), 'Sexism in official statistics'. In J. Irvine *et al.* (eds), *Demystifying Social Statistics*, London, Pluto Press.

OECD (Organisation for Economic Cooperation and Development) (1976), *Data Sources for Social Indicators of Victimization Suffered by Individuals*, OECD Social Indicator Development Programme, Special Study No. 3, Paris.

Office of Population, Censuses and Surveys (1970 and 1980) *Classification of Occupations and Coding Index*, London, HMSO.

Office of Population, Censuses and Surveys, Census Division (1985) CEN 85/1 'Evaluation of the 1981 Census: the 10% sample (bias check)', London, HMSO, June (Census Monitor CEN 85/1).

Ogle, W. (1892), 54th Annual Reports of the Registrar-General, London, HMSO.

Oldman, D. and Illsley, R. (1966), 'Measuring the status of occupations', *Sociological Review*, 14, 1, pp. 53–72.

Pahl, J. (1983) 'The allocation of money and the structuring of inequality within marriages', *Sociological Review*, 31, pp. 237–63.

Pahl, R. E. (1980), 'Employment, work and the domestic division of labour', *International Journal of Labour and Regional Research*, 4(1), pp. 1–20.

Pahl, R. and Wallace, C. (1985), 'Household work strategies in economic recession'. In E. Mingione and N. Redclift (eds), *Beyond Employment*, Oxford, Blackwell.

Parkin, F. (1979), *Marxism and Class Theory: Bourgeois Critique*, London, Tavistock, pp. 14–15.

Parsons, T. (1956), *Family: Socialization and Interaction Process*, London, Routledge & Kegan Paul.

Payne, G. and Payne J. (1981) 'Mobility, employment and the class structure' presented to conference in *Capital and Class*, Dundee, September..

Pearson, K. (1912), 'Social problems: their treatment, past, present and future', Pamphlet, London (available in University of Glasgow library)

Phillips, A. and Taylor, B. (1980), 'Sex and skill: notes towards a feminist analysis', *Feminist Review*, 6, pp. 79–88.

Porter, M. (1983), *Home, Work and Class Consciousness*, Manchester University Press.

Poulten, N. and Heath, A. (1982), 'Women, men and social class'. In E. Gamarnikow *et al.*, *Gender, Class and Work* (1983), London, Heinemann.

Prior, L. (1985) 'Making sense of mortality', *Sociology of Health and Illness* 7(2), pp. 167–90.

Registrar-General (1927) *Decennial Supplement, England and Wales 1921, Part Occupational Mortality*, London, HMSO.

Reid, I. (1981), *Social Class Differences in Britain* (2nd edn), London, Grant MacIntyre.

Reid, I. and Wormald, E. (1982), *Sex Differences in Britain*, London, Grant MacIntyre.

Roberts, H. (1986), 'The social classification of women: a life cycle approach'. Paper presented to a British Sociological Association Conference, Loughborough University.

Roberts, H. (1987), *Women and Social Classification*, Brighton, Wheatsheaf.

Rowntree, B. S. (1937), *The Human Needs of Labour*, London, Longman Green.

Rowntree, B. S. (1941), *Poverty and Progress*, London, Longman, Green.

Rowntree, B. S. (1941) *Poverty and Progress: A Second Social Survey of York*, London, Longman, Green.

Samphier, M. and Thompson, B. (1982), 'The Aberdeen maternity and neo-natal data bank'. In S. A. Medrick and A. E. Baert (eds), *Prospective Longitudinal Research*, Oxford University Press.

Scott-Samuel, A. (1986) 'Social inequalities in health: back on the agenda', *The Lancet*, 10 May 86.

Smith, A. (1793), *The Wealth of Nations*.

Stanworth, M. (1984), 'Women and social class analysis: a reply to Goldthorpe' *Sociology*, 18, pp. 159–70.

Stevenson, T. H. C. (1920) 'The fertility of the various social classes from the middle of the nineteenth century until 1911', *Journal of the Statistical Society*, 83, pp. 401–32.

Stevenson, T. H. C. (1923), 'The social distribution of mortality from different causes in England and Wales, 1910–12', *Biometrika*, XV, pp. 382–400.

Stevenson, T. H. C. (1928), 'The vital statistics of wealth and poverty', *Journal of the Statistical Society*, XCI.

Syson, L. and Young, M. (1974), 'Poverty in Bethnal Green'. In M. Young (ed.), *Poverty Report 1974*, London, Temple Smith.

Szreter, S. R. S. (1984), 'The genesis of the Registrar General's social classification of occupations', *British Journal of Sociology*, XXXV, pp, 522–46.

Thomas, R, and Stanyer, A. (1984) 'Towards statistics for policy making', Social Sciences Occasional Papers, Milton Keynes, The Open University.

Townsend, D. P., Phillimore, P. and Beattie, A. (1986), *Inequalities in Health in the Northern Region*, Report to Northern RHA, Bristol University, Newcastle and Bristol.

Townsend, P. and Davidson, N. (eds) (1982), *Inequalities in Health: The Black Report*, Harmondsworth, Penguin.

United Nations (1989) *Convention for the Right of the Child*. New York, United Nations.

West, P., Macintyre, S., Annandale, E. and Hurst, K. (1990) 'Social class and health in youth: findings from the West of Scotland Twenty-07 Study', *Social Science and Medicine*, 30, 6, pp. 665–73.

Whitehead, A. (1981) 'I'm hungry mum. The politics of domestic budgeting', in K. Young, C. Wolkowitz and R. McCullagh (eds), *Of Marriage and the Market: Women's Subordination in International Perspective*, London, CSE Books.

Whitehead, M. (1987), *The Health Divide: Inequalities in Health in the 1980s*, London, Health Education Authority.

Wilkinson, R. G. (1986), *Class and Health: Research and Longitudinal Data*, London, Tavistock.

Wright, E. O. (1978), *Classes*, London, HMSO.

Young, M. and Willmott, P. (1956), 'Social grading by manual workers', *British Journal of Sociology*, 7, pp. 337–45.

Name Index

Abbott, P. and Sapsford, R. 3, 5, 121
Aberdeen Child Development Survey 70, 71
Arber, S. *et al.* 123

Berent, J. 45
Black Report 56, 67
Blaxter, M. 68
Boston, G. 27
Britten, N. and Heath, A. 123
Brundlandt, C.H., Liestol, K. and Walloe, L. 115
Butler, N.L. and Alberman, E.D. 79, 108

Carr-Hill, R.A. 68, 71, 72, 78, 81, 84, 109, 117
Carr-Hill, R.A. and Pritchard, C. 126
Carr-Hill, R.A., Fraser, C. and Russell, M. 128
Census Report 11, 12, 33, 34
Census and Vital Registration System 13
Classification of Occupations 27
Coleman, D.A. 45
Collett, C.E. 34, 36
Cox, B., Blaxter, N., Buckle, E. *et al.* 67, 77, 82, 129

Dale, A. *et al.* 124
Decennial Supplement 11, 17
Delphy, C. 5
Dex, S. 5
Dowding, V.M. 56, 74
Dunbar, W.C. 18
Duncan, O.D. 61

Erikson, R. 123
Eveleth, P.B. and Tanner, J.M. 76, 128

Floud, R. 109, 128
Fox, A.J. 48, 54

Galton, F. 23, 108
Glass, D.V. 46
Goldblatt, P. 90
Goldthorpe, J. 4, 41, 43, 59, 75, 105, 106
Goldthorpe, J. and Payne, C. 86, 123

Haaga, J., Kenrick, C., Test, K. and Mason, J. 110

Hall, J. and Jones, D.C. 59
Harre, R.L. 61
Hart, N. 60, 68
Haskey, J. 45
Health and Lifestyle Survey 71
Heath, A. 47
Heath, A. and Britten, N. 4, 56
Hindness, B. 2
Hoinville, G. and Jowell, R. 130
Hope, K. and Goldthorpe, J. 59, 61
Humphreys, N.A. 17

Illsley, R. 7, 47, 113, 126
Illsley, R. and Carr-Hill, R.A. 70
Illsley, R. and Mitchell, R.D. 70, 89, 90
Interdepartmental Inquiry on Physical Deterioration 18

Jones, I.G. and Cameron, D. 22

Knight, I. 71, 78, 84, 85, 86, 101, 109, 111

Leete, A. and Fox, J. 10, 17, 18, 25, 36, 64, 105
Lindgren, G. 115

Macintyre, J. 129
Macintyre, S. and West, P. 113
Mcdowell, M. 20, 34, 42, 54, 67
Macfarlane, A. 34
Macfarlane, A. and Mugford, M. 64
Mack, J. and Lansley, J. 69
Martin, J. and Roberts, C. 122
Miles, I. 69
Murgatroyd, L. 123

Nissel, M. 36, 38

Oakley, A. 2, 23
Oakley, A. and Oakley, R. 36
OECD 69
Ogle, W. 18
Ohlin–Wright Scale 61
Oldman, D. and Illsley, R. 59
OPCS 27

Pahl, J. 41, 121, 123
Pahl, R.E. 41, 121, 123

137

Name Index

Pahl, R.C. and Wallace, C. 123
Parkin, F. 5
Parsons, T. 3, 69
Payne, G. and Payne, J. 44
Plowden, L. 67
Poulten, N. and Heath, A. 41
Prior, L. 130

Reading Survey 89
Reid, I. 1
Reid, I. and Wormald, E. 67
Roberts, H. 122
Rowntree, B.S. 23

Samphier, M. and Thompson, B. 70
Smith, A. 18
Stanworth, N. 4

Stevenson, T.H.C. 5, 6, 35 (and Chs 2, 6, 11 *passim*)
Syson, L. and Young, M. 41
Szreter, S.R.S. 5, 17—20, 22, 120

Thomas, and Stanyer, A. 27
Townsend, P. and Davidson, N. 56, 67, 111
Townsend, D.P., Phillimore, P. and Beattie, A. 58
Torgenson, R. 115

West, P. *et al.* 112
Whitehead, A. 30, 41, 67, 68
Wilkinson, R.G. 30, 60

Young, M. and Wilmott, P. 68

Subject Index

Aberdeen
  Child Development Survey 70, 71
  Market Research Classification 10
  Maternity and Neo-Natal Data
    Bank xiii, 6, 46, 64, 70–2, 74, 79, 80, 83, 87, 88, 91–7, 115
  MRC Medical Sociology Unit 70
Age of women
  and birth 64, 65
  early adulthood 110–12
  and employment 40, 122
  and fertility 35, 64
  and first pregnancy 65
  middle-age 109
  and social class 63, 121

Birth 86–98, 126
  and birthweight 90, 96
  first time 64–5
  illegimate 11
  legitimate 11, 12
  premature 92–5
Boer wars 18
  class theory 3–5, 59, 61
  classification criteria 6, 56–61, 124–5
  'culture' (T.H.C. Stevenson) 14–15, 16, 42, 43

Contraception 64

Educational attainment 61, 62, 67, 69, 71, 75, 80–2, 88, 126,
Employment
  and leisure 72
  attitudes to women's 4, 33, 38, 45
  unemployment 58
  women's 4, 33, 34, 37, 38, 40, 46, 58, 72, 122
Ethnic minorities 58
Eugenicism *see* Hereditarianism

Fertility
  differentials of class 18–19, 31
  occupational and class 11, 13, 16, 35, 54, 63–7, 118
General Registry Office 11, 17, 18, 33, 34
Geographical mobility 40

Health 18, 20, 23, 39, 71, 76–80, 84–6, 89–92, 102, 109–13
  class inequalities 12, 13, 16, 18–19, 55, 56, 63–6, 125
  historical Ch. 2 *passim*, 32
  psychological 80–82
Height
  of men 7, Ch. 9 *passim*, 109, 127
  of women: and birthweight 63, 88–90, 96, 126; and education 80–2, 86; and feasibility of social class indicator 6–7, 54–5, 62–6, 74, 76–98, 101, 105, 107–9, 113, 115, 116, 126, 127; and fertility and mortality 54, 64–6, 67; and health 52, 76–8, 84–6, 89–92, 102, 103, 108–13; and housing tenure 84, 105; and life chances 69–76; and pre-nuptial conception 86–7, 93, 95; and smoking/alcohol use 85, 86, 93, 94
Homogamy
  class 44–52, 120–1
  height 106
HORG 6, 7, 52, 54, Ch. 6 *passim*, 67, 73, 75–7, 80, 89, 90, 97, 98, 100, Ch. 9 *passim*, 109, 113, 119, 121, 127
Housing tenure 57, 62, 69, 83, 84, 105

Income 14, 41, 61, 62
International labour office 30
IQ 73, 88, 89

Life chances
  general 57, 63, 68
  of women 41, 42, 55, 63, 70, 73, Ch. 8
Low birthweight study (1970) 70

Marriage
  and divorce 67
  patterns of 3, 4, 36, 37, 38, 42, 43, Ch. 5 *passim*, 86, 100, 105, 113
  status and head of household 36–8, 40–2, 57, 58, 75, 120
Marxist standpoint 2, 59
Material wealth and social class 11–17, 32, 41, 62, 72, 75, 82, 83, 124, 126
Measuring inequalities Part II *passim*, 113, 124

Subject Index

of men 2, 4
of women 1, 3–7, Ch. 9 *passim*, 117, 118
discriminating power and 6, Part II *passim*, 120, 125, 127–9
Methodology and attendant problems Ch. 2 *passim*, 31, 32, 54, 55, 56–61, 67–9, 75–6, 96–8, Ch. 11 *passim*
Morbidity 48, 71, 129
Mortality 16, 17, 18, 21–3, 34, 42, 57, 63, 64, 66, 68, 69, 120
of infants 11, 16, 17, 34, 54, 64, 66, 67, 110, 118
of women 34, 36
of men 35, 36, 118
perinatal 59, 64

Occupation Ch. 2 *passim*, 30–2, 33–7, 40–3, 55, 57, 58, 68, 105, 118, 119, 122
and classification of women 1, 33–8, 54, 55, 44, 58, 62, 68, 69, 75, 105, 118, 120, 122–4
and classification of men 11–13, 26–29, 44, 75, 105, 117
and 'culture' 14, 15, 16, 42, 46, 47, 128
and opportunity/mobility 15, 46, 75, 89, 120, 122
and mortality of women 34, 57, 58
and general mortality 57, 58
and reclassifications 13–15, 27–30, 46, 58, 126
education and training 25, 30, 62, 75
housework 122
of women with children 122
part-time 122
tripartite division 12, 15, 44, 5

Pregnancy (and related) 54, 63, 64, 70, 71, 79, 95, 97
and pre-eclampsia 90, 91
and prenuptial conception 86, 93
Public social provision 18, 18, 69, 72
third world 108, 109, 128

Quality of life 6, 41, 69, 70, 71–4, 124–5

Registrar-General's social class scheme 5, 10–23, 31, 32, 33, 34–7, 41–3, 44–6, 56–9, 61–4, 68, 69, 72–4, 75, 76, 78, 80, 83, 108, 113, 118–21, 123–7, 130

Social classification (general) Ch. 2 *passim*, 56, 57, 58, 59, 63, 67, 75, Ch. 11 *passim*
according to head of household 33, 37, 119, 120
and economic power 3, 17, 27, 41, 61, 131
and maternal height 62–6, 67, 74, 79–80, 86–93, 96–8
changes of status 25–30, 122
feminist analysis and critique 5
geographical variables 13, 85
of family/household 3, 4, 13, 14, 36–8, 40–3, 47, 82, 105, 107, 122, 123
of men 15, 31, 42, 43, 44, 47, 64, 66, 75–81, 83–9, 120
of unmarried women 10, 37, 40, 58, 61, 67, 97
of women 4, Ch. 4 *passim*, 44–6, 54, 55, 62, 63, 75, 113, Ch. 11 *passim*
of women according to associated men 3–5, 10, 33, 35, 38–40, 42–6, 57–9, 64–6, Ch. 8 *passim*, 100, 101, 103–7, 113, 118, 120, 127
origins and history 5, Ch. 2 *passim*, 25–31, 33, 36
stratification theory 3, 5, 69, 113
theoretical and ideological 2, 17–23, 27, 31, 57–60, 67–9, 100, Ch. 11 *passim*
Social mobility 59, 113–4
Social structure, analysis of: hereditarian v. environmentalist 18–20, 22
Surrey university 124
Sweden 43

Tenure (housing) 61, 62

Weberian 3, 59, 131

ACX-0986